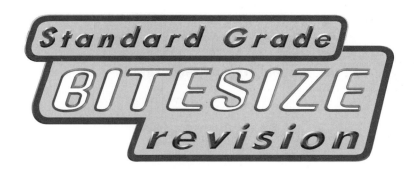

Standard Grade BITESIZE revision

History

Tom Monaghan

Principal Teacher, Social Subjects

With thanks to Allan Todd, author of GCSE Bitesize Revision:
Modern World History, first published 1998, reprinted 1999,
and Don Esson, Principal Teacher of History at Nairn Academy.

Contents

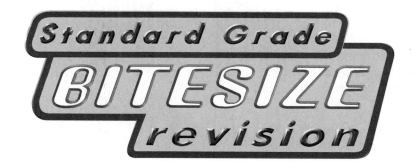

BBC

Picture credits

Every effort has been made to trace the copyright holders of material used
in this book. If, however, any omissions have been made, we would be
happy to rectify this at the earliest opportunity. Please contact us at the
address below.

Published by BBC Educational Publishing, BBC White City,
201 Wood Lane, London W12 7TS
First published 2000, Reprinted 2001
© Tom Monaghan/BBC Worldwide (Educational Publishing), 2000

ISBN: 0 563 47493 9

Designed by Linda Reed and Associates.

Printed in Great Britain by Bell & Bain Ltd., Glasgow

About BITESIZE History

BITESIZE History is a revision guide that has been specially put together to help you with your Standard Grade exams. You can tape the TV programmes and watch them on video, work your way through the activities and suggestions in this book, and dial up the Internet online service.

It's called BITESIZE History because it's been divided into manageable bitesize pieces of revision – much better than doing hours of revision in the days before the exam! The video, which gives you information and advice, can be watched as often as you like until you have understood all of the points. Many sections of the video tie in with sections in this book, but it is not necessary to use the video and you can use the book by itself quite effectively. The sections in the book are divided into subsections that you can work through one by one. If you still do not understand something, you can contact the online team at 'Ask a Teacher' who are there to help you.

How to use this book

The book is divided into ten sections that cover the ten contexts that can be studied at Standard Grade. If you have any doubts about which topics you have covered, ask your teacher.

Each section of the book follows a similar pattern:

- an **introduction** page that lists the main content that can be set in the examination. It tells you about the particular type of question that you will be practising, as well as the topics being covered in the FactZones

- a **FactZone** that give more detailed historical information about the topics from the most popular contexts

- every context has at least one page of **exam-type questions** at **General** and/or **Credit** levels on some of the topics – usually there are one or two practice questions, with tips to help you to understand what the examiner is looking for, and hints to help you to answer similar questions in other units.

For many of the sections, there are corresponding sections on the video. The video sequences give extra information and tips on how to answer exam questions. You could write the time codes from the video on the relevant page(s) of the book – this will help you to find the video sequences quickly as you go over the sections again.

Important topics of the Standard Grade History syllabus that many candidates find difficult are covered by the book, but Bitesize History doesn't aim to provide total coverage of all topics. Therefore, it's important to use your own school text book and notes to revise as well.

KEY TO SYMBOLS

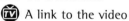 A link to the video

? Something to think about

◎ An activity to do

🖱 A link to the website

f Foundation Level

g General Level

c Credit Level

The information in each section of this book should help you to keep a record of topics that you have covered and revised thoroughly. At the same time, because the main types of Standard Grade History question are covered, the general tips and advice in this book will be useful, even when some of your topics are not covered by FactZones. Remember that the skills required to answer Knowledge and Understanding and Enquiry Skills questions are transferable to the content of any topic.

The activities suggested in the book include:

- highlighting (either with highlighter pens, or by underlining or circling) certain words and phrases in the sources and/or in the information that accompanies the sources (e.g. the date, country of origin, author). This activity encourages you to look closely at the sources and their details of origin. This is something that you could usefully do on your examination papers to make sure that you do not miss any important points.

- writing – either Knowledge and Understanding or Enquiry Skills questions.

Taken together, the book, video and online resources cover much of the content and all of the main skills required to achieve a good grade in Standard Grade History.

About Standard Grade History

You have to complete **three** units of study for Standard Grade History. Each unit focuses on a broad theme:

- Changing Life

- Co-operation and Conflict

- People and Power

Unit I looks at **Changing Life**: changing life in Scotland and Britain, concentrating on social, economic and political changes in the period from 1750 to the present day. There are three contexts (you study one of them):

A 1750s-1850s   B 1830s-1930s   C 1880s-present day

Unit II looks at **Co-operation and Conflict**: international co-operation and conflict in the period from 1790 to the 1960s. There are three contexts (again, you study one of them):

A 1790s- 1820s   B 1890s-1920s   C 1930s-1960s

Unit III looks at People and Power: struggles for power and political dominance within specific countries. There are four contexts (once again, you study one of them):

A USA 1850-1880   B India 1917-1947

C Russia 1914-1941   D Germany 1918-1939

THE ONLINE SERVICE You can find extra support, tips and answers to your exam queries on the Standard Grade BITESIZE website. The address is www.bbc.co.uk/ scotland/revision

The final examination

There are **two** elements that are assessed in the final examination:

- Knowledge and Understanding
- Enquiry Skills.

The final examination leads to an overall award on a 7-point scale of grades for both elements: grade 1 is the highest. Your certificate will record your attainment in both assessable elements as well as giving you an overall award for Standard Grade History. Your overall award is an aggregate of the element grades, with Knowledge and Understanding and Enquiry Skills being weighted 40:60, e.g. Knowledge and Understanding 2, Enquiry Skills 1 = Overall 1.

Three papers are set each year at **Foundation**, **General** and **Credit** Levels.

Paper	Grades	Units	Time allocation
Foundation	6 & 5	I and either II or III*	1 hour
General	4 & 3	I, II and III	1 hour 30 minutes
Credit	2 & 1	I, II and III	1 hour 45 minutes

* At Foundation Level, Unit I is assessed every year, and you will be notified of the other unit to be assessed in January of S.4, through your school or presenting centre.

How to revise Standard Grade History

There are three main aspects to successful revision, as opposed to unplanned, unfocused and therefore unsuccessful revision! These are:

- **organise**: prepare a long-term revision plan, in order to make most of your time
- **learn**: make sure that you know the relevant facts
- **apply**: understand and practise how to answer different types of question.

Organise

You need to draw up a revision timetable to cover all of your subjects – not just History! It should begin three or four months (not weeks or days!) before your exams start. Once you have drawn up an outline timetable, divide the days (say 90 or 100) by the number of subjects your sitting. This will tell you how many days you have for revising History. Try to remember these three very important points about revising.

1. Don't try to revise for more than 40 minutes at a time, otherwise you may overload your brain! About three 40-minute sessions per night is enough for most people. Make sure that your plan includes breaks (of at least 10-15 minutes) between each session.

2. Be realistic – build in time off for activities such as sport, the cinema or visiting friends and relatives. One complete day off and one night off each week is reasonable. If you start early enough, and you revise hard, you should be able to persuade your parents that some time off is okay!

3. Try to stick to your plan. Should illness, for example, disrupt it, try to reorganise your plan to take account of this. Also, if you start early enough, you can get round problems like this without having to panic.

Learn

This is much harder – and less pleasant – than drawing up a revision timetable. First of all, make sure that you know the exam requirements (such as number of units, types of exam paper, length of exam paper). Read over the section on the exam in this book and check with your teacher. Instead of rewriting your notes several times over or simply reading your text book, try some other revision methods:

- highlight or underline key words, terms, names and facts in your notes

- write these highlighted words onto index cards

- draw spider diagrams or mind maps

- listen to cassette recordings of you (or a friend or relative) reading out the main points

- ask someone to test you on a topic, or try one of the Test Bites on the Bitesize website

- make visual displays of the main points of a unit on a piece of A3 or A4 paper, with brief facts in boxes, as in this example.

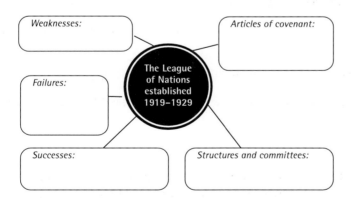

These diagrams can be highlighted or underlined to help your memory. You can put them on your bedroom wall. You should be able to cover most topics in your three units on four or five pages, at most.

Whatever revision methods you use, make sure that you revise in a warm, quiet room, away from all distractions. Try to keep your revision varied. For example, use a combination of note-making on cards, highlighting, writing fuller notes and attempting exam-type questions.

Apply

It is as important to practise answering the different types of question as it is to learn the facts. For one revision session, you could read through the FactZone on a topic, watch a video sequence (if there is one) and then work through the example question. In your next revision session, you could read through the FactZone, highlighting key words, phrases etc., then write out some revision cards before tackling the second practice question, making sure that you follow the suggestions given. In particular, make sure that you are familiar with and practise the full range of Knowledge and Understanding and Enquiry Skills questions that will be asked.

Knowledge and Understanding

You have to demonstrate **three** different skills by answering three different types of Knowledge and Understanding question. You will be asked to:

- give an account of an event or development, e.g. describe something that happened

- give an explanation of the causes or consequences of an event, development, action and/or attitude, e.g. give reasons for some development

- give and support a view about the importance of an event, development, action or attitude, e.g. say how important you think someone or some event was.

In the Knowledge and Understanding questions, you should use whatever you already know in your answer. At General level, this means at least one piece of your own information. At Credit level, you'll have to rely on what you've already learned as nothing is provided by way of source material or information to help you answer.

Enquiry Skills

There are **six** Enquiry Skills. They are the same at General and Credit levels. Here is a list of what you are expected to be able to do:

- decide if a source is or is not useful, reliable or valuable: remember that a biased or unreliable source can be useful, e.g. as evidence of how people thought or as an example of propaganda

- explain the point of view in a source, i.e. the **attitude** or **opinion** of the author(s) and the evidence or **reasons** for this

- compare the evidence in more than one source, e.g. where they **agree** or **disagree**, and the **evidence** or **reasons** for this or the **usefulness** or **value** of two sources

- find and organise evidence from two or more sources (only asked in Unit I)

- come to a balanced conclusion about an issue, **using the evidence in the sources** provided and **your own knowledge** (only asked in Unit I)

- show that you know what was going on at the time a source was produced ('setting source in context') using **your own knowledge, as well as the evidence in the source** (only asked in Units II and III).

Remember that for most Enquiry Skills questions, all of the evidence that you need will be found in the sources and in the introductions to them. Where you need to use your own knowledge to get full marks, this will be clearly indicated in the question.

Do not hesitate to use your own knowledge in Enquiry Skills questions, even when it is not asked for, so long as you don't forget to use the evidence in the sources.

On the day

Make sure that you know what sections you have studied. If in doubt, ask before the exam begins! Note carefully the total time you plan to spend on each question, giving more time to questions with the highest marks.

When there is a choice of questions, read over each one carefully to make sure that you choose the question that you know the most about. For the short essay question at Credit level, make a rough plan first – it is important to find out right at the beginning whether or not you know enough about the topic (if not, it gives you time to select the other topic). A plan also gives you something to note down should you get into serious time trouble – you will get some marks for a note-style answer.

Some teachers suggest that you should answer the Enquiry Skills questions in each unit first. This is because they are worth more marks than the Knowledge and Understanding questions. This is a good idea as long as you remember to answer all of the questions, and clearly label your answers so that you do not confuse the marker. Try to leave some time at the end to check over your answers for careless mistakes.

Finally, don't panic. As long as you have followed your teacher's advice, and the suggestions in this book and in the video, you will be well-prepared for any questions that the examiner can think up.

Remember that the exam is not meant to catch you out: it is designed to let you show off what you know, understand and can do.

Good luck!

12

g **C** To be able to answer questions on Changing life in Scotland and Britain 1750-1850s, you should know about the following:

Population growth and distribution
- reasons for growth
- redistribution in the countryside and towns
- changes in the Highlands (clearances and emigration)

Technological change and its effects
- developments in agriculture
- developments in the textile industry

Changes in employment and in working conditions
- on the land
- in textile factories

Changes in social conditions
- health and housing in rural and urban areas

Parliamentary reform in Scotland and England
- franchise and representation before and after 1832
- radical unrest at Bonnymuir and Peterloo.

f To be able to answer questions on Changing life in Scotland and Britain 1750-1850s, you should know about the following:

Population growth and distribution
- reasons for population growth and distribution
- Highland clearances

Technological change and its effects
- developments in the textile industry

Changes in employment and in working conditions
- in textile factories

Changes in social conditions
- health and housing in towns

Parliamentary reform in Scotland and England
- franchise and representation before and after 1832
- radical unrest at Bonnymuir.

The FactZones look at the House of Commons before 1832 and radical unrest 1819-1820.

The practice questions and the mini-investigation are set at General level.

FactZONE

You need to learn these key facts:

The House of Commons before 1832

Franchise or voting qualification

In England and Wales, the qualification needed to vote was different in the 40 counties and more than 200 boroughs.

In counties, male 'freeholders' who possessed land valued at 40 shillings (£1.60) could vote. In boroughs, there were six main types of qualification: Scot and Lot, Potwalloper, Burgage, Corporation, Freeman and Freeholder. Few people could vote in boroughs.

At the end of the eighteenth century, there were 149 boroughs with fewer than 500 voters, and only 54 boroughs with more than 500 voters.

Scotland

In Scotland, the qualification in 33 counties was supposed to be similar to that in England and Wales, but there were less than 1400 Scots qualified to vote in the counties. There were 33 counties, with 27 counties having one MP each, and 6 taking it in turn to elect 3 Members of Parliament at every second election.

Scottish cities and burghs were combined into groups of four or five, apart from Edinburgh as the capital city. Voting was restricted to members of burgh councils, e.g. Glasgow (population 75 000) shared a Member of Parliament with Renfrew (population 2000), Rutherglen (population 2400) and Dumbarton (population 2500), selected by four delegates chosen by each of the burgh councils! Glasgow's delegate was chosen by the 32 members of the council.

4000 voters, out of a population of more than two million, elected Scotland's 45 Members of Parliament.

Elections

In England and Wales, there were 56 nomination or rotten boroughs with little or no population sending more than 100 representatives or Members to Parliament.

There were many pocket boroughs where the local landowner controlled the election. There was no secret voting (or ballot) and as voting took place in public, bribery and intimidation were common. General Elections could take up to two weeks to be completed.

Henry Dundas (Ist Viscount Melville)

For nearly thirty years, Dundas was the most powerful man in Scotland. He was known as 'Harry the Ninth' and the 'Uncrowned King of Scotland' because he was able to influence the election of Members of Parliament, and find government jobs for his friends, relatives and political supporters. In 1802, he was chiefly responsible for the election of 43 Tory MPs in Scotland, out of 45 constituencies. This delighted the Tory Prime Minister, Addington. Dundas died in 1811.

You need to learn these key facts:

Radical unrest 1819–1820

'Peterloo' (1819)

This is the name given to the incident that took place at St Peter's Fields in Manchester on the 16 August 1819. 'Peterloo' is a mocking reference to the actions of the local yeomanry or part-time soldiers whose actions contrasted with the bravery of the troops who fought the French at Waterloo four years earlier.

Local magistrates decided to arrest Henry Hunt who was speaking to around 80 000 people at a meeting in support of political reform. This decision led to cavalry belonging to the Manchester and Salford Yeomanry charging into the crowd. Fifteen unarmed civilians were killed and over four hundred were injured. Henry Hunt was arrested and sentenced to two years in prison.

The Home Secretary sent a letter of congratulation to the Manchester magistrates whose actions had led to the deaths and injuries.

Bonnymuir (1820)

Radicals demanded parliamentary reform despite the repressive measures taken by the government to deal with its opponents. Radical support was strong in Scotland due to rising prices, high taxes and unemployment among handloom weavers and farm labourers.

In February 1820, the government arrested 27 members of a Glasgow radical group suspected of planning a rising against the government in Scotland and England.

A strike in Glasgow led to a group of forty or fifty radicals marching to the Carron Iron Works near Falkirk where weapons were manufactured. They hoped to steal enough weapons to arm the strikers in Glasgow.

Government troops attacked the marchers at Bonnymuir. Four of the radicals were wounded and the rest were rounded up and taken into custody.

At the same time, a small group of radicals marched from Strathaven to Glasgow. Their march was halted by the authorities, too. Fifty prisoners who were accused of leading the 'insurrection' were tried for treason. John Baird, Andrew Hardie and James Wilson were sentenced to public execution. Nineteen others were transported to Australia.

Radical reform

Radicals demanded electoral reforms such as universal suffrage (votes for all men, at least), annual parliaments (frequent elections would make bribery too expensive) and secret ballots (corrupt politicians would not be able to find out if people who had taken their money had voted for them). The campaign for radical reform of the electoral system continued after the 1832 parliamentary reforms, through the Chartist movement.

Knowledge and Understanding

Parliamentary reform

> Before 1832, about 4000 voters out of a population of more than two million elected Scotland's 45 Members of Parliament. There were less than 1400 Scots qualified to vote in the counties. Apart from Edinburgh as the capital city, Scottish cities and burghs were combined into groups of four or five. Voting was restricted to members of burgh councils.

◎ *ℊ* *Why did the radicals want Parliament to be reformed? (4)*

You need to identify three reasons from the source to be awarded three marks. You need to be able to identify another reason from recalled knowledge to be awarded the full four marks, e.g. six Scottish counties took it in turns to elect three MPs at every second General Election; voting took place in public, encouraging bribery, corruption and intimidation.

You should be familiar with the term 'radicals' used to describe people who demanded a wide range of reforms, including the reform of Parliament.

REMEMBER
When you revise, organise your notes and handouts into three sections, one for each unit, and then divide the notes for each unit into the main headings that you have covered.

Enquiry Skills

The Enquiry Skills questions in Unit I are supposed to test the skills needed to complete a mini-investigation into an issue, e.g. farming methods in Scotland changed during the period 1750-1800.

At Foundation, General and Credit levels, the Enquiry Skills section in Unit I will have a sub-heading that says:

The issue for investigating is:

Then there will be a box containing the issue to be investigated. Below the box it will say:

Study the sources carefully and answer the questions which follow.

You should use your own knowledge where appropriate.

The sources and questions will follow.

REMEMBER
At Credit level, try to practise writing answers to the short essay questions (setting aside no more than 10-15 minutes for each answer).

Practice mini-investigation

Farming methods

⑨ The issue for investigating is: farming methods in Scotland changed during the period 1750-1800.

Study the sources carefully and answer the questions which follow. You should use your own knowledge where appropriate.

Source A is taken from a description of farming methods in Berwickshire published in 1797.

> *Wheat, oats, barley, turnips, potatoes are here cultivated with a success which even the richest counties in England might envy. The subdivision and enclosure of fields; the rotation of crops, adopted for the purpose of continually enjoying, yet without exhausting the fertility of the soil; the choice of seeds; the culture of the ground by tillage, manuring, weeding, watering ... distinguish the shire of Berwick as a district in which agriculture has been happily carried to high perfection.*
>
> **A**

◎ *How useful is Source A for investigating changes in farming methods in Scotland during the period 1750-1800? (3)*

? *Pick out useful evidence of farming change in the source: references to enclosed fields, crop rotation, selection of seeds etc.*

? *Consider whether the author is biased when he refers to Berwickshire possibly being the envy of the richest counties in England.*

? C *Think about issues such as who wrote the source, when it was written, whether it contain fact and/or opinion etc.*

As a rule, most sources will be 'quite useful', with strengths and weaknesses; there will be plenty of things to write about.

Remember to use the information in the introduction to the source: it describes farming in Berwickshire in 1797 (at the end of the period 1750-1800); Berwickshire is only one county in Scotland.

C At Credit level

■ Do **not** say that a source is useful because it was 'written by a man who was there at the time' or 'it is a primary source' – say **who** the author is (if it is known); where the author was writing (if known) and when the author was writing (as accurately as possible).

■ Your evaluation should be **balanced**, i.e. the sources are quite useful because they have strengths and weaknesses.

Source B is taken from an account of farming in the Highlands written in 1794.

> B
>
> Many cattle and sheep died in winter because of the shortage of grass and hay: even in late April, the country at large lay a mere waste; nothing to be seen but stones and dry blades of couch grass; the pasture and meadow lands gnawed to the quick, and strewed with the dead carcasses of sheep.

◎ *What evidence in Source A agrees with the view that farming methods in Scotland changed in the period 1750-1800?*

What evidence in Source B disagrees with the view that farming methods in Scotland changed in the period 1750-1800? (5)

Do not use recalled information.

You must answer both parts of the question. You can draw a simple table with two columns: one 'for' (evidence from Source A) and one 'against' (evidence from Source B).

Remember that this question is simply asking you to select and organise information so you do not have to waste valuable time trying to put brief extracts from the sources into your own words.

REMEMBER
At Credit level, if you don't use the sources, use recalled information or reach a balanced conclusion, you cannot gain good marks.

C At Credit level

■ You must identify where the evidence comes from, e.g. in brackets, say that it comes from Source A, B or C.

■ Simply writing down the evidence may not be enough – you may have to explain that the evidence suggests or hints that there were other factors.

? *Look at the practice question below. Think about how you can come to a balanced conclusion dealing with both sides of the issue, e.g. working conditions improved for some people but not for others (this is not necessary at General level, but is good practice for General/Credit level candidates).*

? *What recalled information, i.e. relevant evidence that is not in the sources, could you use to answer the practice question below?*

Practice question

■ How far do you agree that farming methods in Scotland changed in the period 1750-1800? You must use evidence from the sources and your own knowledge to come to a conclusion. (4)

Write one or two paragraphs to answer this question. Allow yourself 10 minutes.

Context B: 1830s-1930s

C g To be able to answer questions on Changing life in Scotland and Britain 1830s-1930s, you should know about the following:

Population growth and distribution
- reasons for growth
- redistribution in the countryside and towns
- Highland migration within the UK and emigration
- Irish migration to Scotland

Technological change and its effects
- developments in coal mining
- developments in railways

Changes in employment and working conditions
- on the land
- in the coal mines

Changes in social conditions
- health and housing in rural and urban areas

Parliamentary reform in Scotland and England
- the extension of the franchise, 1867-1928
- the movement for Women's Suffrage, 1890s-1928

f To be able to answer questions on Changing life in Scotland and Britain 1830s-1930s, you should know about the following:

Population growth and distribution
- reasons for population growth and distribution
- emigration from the Highlands

Technological change and its effects
- developments in coal mining

Changes in employment and working conditions
- in the coal mines

Changes in social conditions
- health and housing in towns

Parliamentary reform in Scotland and England
- the Suffragette Movement, 1903-1914

The FactZone looks at parliamentary reform, 1867-1928.

The practice questions focus on the mini-investigation at Credit level.

FactZONE

Parliamentary reform 1867–1928

This is a summary of the main factors and developments that you should have covered in class:
- basic background to how the parliamentary system works in the UK
- problems with the parliamentary system before 1867
- details of the main reforms that helped to make the UK a more democratic country
(see timeline below)
- background to Women's Suffrage movements
- details of the leadership, aims and tactics of the Suffragettes up to 1914
- the role played by women during the First World War and its impact on women being given the right to vote in 1918
- the terms of the 1918 and 1928 Acts.

Problems with the parliamentary system before 1867

- Only a small percentage of males could vote (90% of the population could not vote and no females were allowed to vote at all).
- The non-elected House of Lords was much more powerful than it is today.
- Only wealthy, property-owning males could become MPs (there was a property qualification for candidates and MPs were not paid).
- Constituencies varied greatly in size of population.
- Voting took place in public at the 'hustings' and the small number of voters could be influenced by the three 'Bs': bribery, bullying and blackmail.
- General Elections only needed to take place every seven years.

Timeline

1832 The Reform Act standardised voting qualifications in many constituencies and improved the distribution of MPs in some parts of the country.
1867 Second Reform Act (and **Scotland, 1868**) increased the number of voters and made further improvements to the distribution of MPs.
1872 Ballot Act meant that voting took place in secret, reducing corruption at elections.
1884 Representation of the People Act doubled the number of voters from two and a half million to five million males.
1885 Redistribution of Seats Act continued the redistribution of seats started in 1832 and 1867, making constituencies more equal in terms of number of voters and creating more single member constituencies.
1911 Parliament Act reduced the power of the non-elected House of Lords; General Elections had to take place at least every five years.
1911 Payment of MPs enabled a wider range of candidates from less wealthy backgrounds to stand for election (not only working-class MPs sponsored by trade unions or other movements).
1918 Representation of the People Act extended the right to vote to all men over 21 and all women over 30; General Elections to be held on a single day.
1928 Representation of the People (Equal Franchise) Act granted the right to vote to women over 21, on equal terms to men.

Practice mini-investigation

Population growth

For more about Enquiry Skills and the mini-investigation section, see page 15.

C The issue for investigating is: the growth of industry led to the increase in the population of Scotland's towns and cities between 1830 and 1900.

Study the sources carefully and answer the questions which follow. You should use your own knowledge where appropriate.

Source A was written by someone living in Glasgow in 1838.

> *There are people who have come to Glasgow from as far as 60 miles away. My own father was a farmer in the Lothians. He was driven out by improvements in farming so he became a mechanic and settled in Glasgow. When small farms disappeared, many cottagers were driven out and they moved to the large towns.*

A

Source B was written by the historian T. C. Smout.

> Glasgow was by far the largest of Scotland's great towns, and it was experiencing a headlong rate of increase: at 275,000 it was twelve times as large as it had been in 1775, and between 1831 and 1841 it had grown by more than one-third. Edinburgh, at 138,000, was now only half Glasgow's size ... Aberdeen, Dundee and Paisley were about half the size of the capital, at 60-65,000. Yet – and the point is an important one – only 35% of the population lived in towns of over 5,000 inhabitants.

B

Source C is from 'The Irish in Scotland' published in 1947.

> *The coal, iron and textile industries (of Glasgow and Lanarkshire) attracted tens of thousands of immigrants in search of work. ...With this expansion of Glasgow came the growth of the Irish population ...The decline of the linen and woollen industries in the north of Ireland and the rise of the cotton industry in the west of Scotland attracted Irish towards the city.*

> **REMEMBER**
> In the exam, you should plan to spend more time on questions worth more marks.

Practice questions

1 How useful are Sources A and B for investigating whether industrial growth was responsible for the rise in population of Scotland's towns and cities? (4)

■ Make sure you actually answer the question by writing something like 'Source A is useful because ... ' and 'Source B is useful because ... '

■ Remember to write about both sources.

■ Relate your answer to the whole question, i.e. are the sources useful for investigating the reasons for the growth in the population of Scotland's towns and cities?

■ The sources' content is important, but think about issues such as who wrote the sources, when they were written, whether they contain fact and/or opinion etc.

■ Remember that a secondary source could be more useful than a primary source if it contains more accurate and reliable information when that is what you are looking for. At other times, you may be looking for sources that tell you what people were thinking and unreliable primary sources are what you need.

2 What evidence in the sources supports the view that industrial growth was responsible for the rise in population of Scotland's towns and cities?

What evidence in the sources suggests that industrial growth was not the only reason for the population rise in towns and cities? (6)

3 To what extent did the growth of industry lead to the increase in the population of Scotland's towns and cities between 1830 and 1900?

You must use evidence from the sources and your own knowledge to reach a balanced conclusion. (5)

Allow yourself 20 minutes to answer each of these questions.

Context C: 1880s – present day

g **c** To be able to answer questions on Changing life in Scotland and Britain 1880s-present day, you should know about the following:

Population growth and distribution
- reasons for growth
- redistribution in the countryside and towns
- immigration to, and emigration from, Scotland

Technological change and its effects
- developments in shipbuilding
- developments in road transport

Changes in employment and working conditions
- for women
- the role of trade unions

Changes in social conditions
- health and housing in rural and urban areas

Parliamentary reform in Scotland and England
- the extension of the franchise in the twentieth century
- the movement for Women's Suffrage, 1890s-1928

f To be able to answer questions on Changing life in Scotland and Britain 1880s-present day, you should know about the following:

Population growth and distribution
- reasons for population growth and distribution
- emigration from Scotland

Technological change and its effects
- developments in road transport

Changes in employment and working conditions
- for women

Changes in social conditions
- health and housing in towns

Parliamentary reform in Scotland and England
- the Suffragette Movement, 1903-1914

The FactZones look at changes in employment and working conditions for women and parliamentary reform in Scotland and England after 1884.

The practice questions focus on the mini-investigation at General level.

FactZONE

Women and work before the First World War

■ The largest group of women workers were employed in domestic service. They worked long hours for low wages and often had to live in the homes of their employers.

■ A large number of women also worked in the textile industry and 'sweated industries' such as shirt-making and shoe-stitching. Working hours were long and pay was very low.

■ Some women worked in heavier jobs such as brick-making and chain-making while an increasing number had found work in offices.

■ Some middle-class women went to university. As a result, they began to enter some of the professions such as teaching and medicine.

■ Working women were paid less than men even if they did the same jobs. Middle- and upper-class women were expected to marry, then look after their families and homes.

Women and the First World War

■ During the war, women did important and dangerous work in munitions factories. They took over jobs in public transport, farming, nursing and the Civil Service and joined the armed forces in non-combatant positions. Women's pay increased during the war.

Women and work in the inter-war period

■ Many women lost their jobs when the war ended and men returned home although there were more job opportunities for women in the 1920s and 1930s due to better education. Many women found work as clerks, teachers and nurses. Industries changed: women found work in the new light industries, e.g. making electrical and other consumer goods.

■ **The Sex Disqualification Removal Act of 1919** opened all professions to women apart from the Church. Discrimination prevented many women from remaining at work after marriage, e.g. the Civil Service did not allow women to work after marriage. But by the 1930s, about one-third of housewives in Britain had a job outside the home.

Women and work, 1945-1960s

■ Women carried out vital war work during World War Two. Many learned skills which helped them to find work after the war was over. Light industries such as electronics continued to grow and provided many job opportunities for women.

■ Service industries such as banking grew and provided many jobs for women. Many women found work in the new welfare services set up in the 1940s, such as the National Health Service.

■ Women were paid less than men even if they did the same jobs. A few employers introduced equal pay for women, e.g. women's wages in the Civil Service and teaching matched men's wages by 1961.

Practice mini-investigation

📺 ⊚ Women and work

For more about the Enquiry Skills and mini-investigations section, see page 15.

g The issue for investigating is: working conditions for women at home improved during the 1930s.

Study the sources carefully and answer the questions which follow. You should use your own knowledge where appropriate.

In **Source A** a woman remembers her life in Edinburgh in the 1930s.

> My mother decided to buy a washing machine just before the war broke out. It must have been one of the first in the street.
> Also, we bought an electric fire to heat up the children's bedroom in winter. It was much less trouble than lighting a fire every night. The fire was switched on twenty minutes before we went to bed.
>
> A

❗ REMEMBER Source content is important, but you should also think about issues such as who wrote the source (if it is known), when it was written (if known) and whether it contains fact and/or opinion etc.

◎ *How useful is Source A for investigating the working conditions of women at home between 1930 and 1939? (3)*

⑦ *Pick out useful evidence in the source: the time and effort saved by the washing machine; the fact that the electric fire meant one less fire to light; that there was less coal and ash to carry in and out of the house.*

Remember to use the information in the introduction to the source: it is a woman describing housework at a time when most men didn't help around the house; she lives in a city like so many Scots at that time; she is describing her life in the 1930s.

Consider that the woman's memories are not typical of most Scots at that time ('one of the first in the street'); at the same time, she provides evidence that new consumer goods, such as washing machines and electric fires, were being bought by some people.

Source B describes life in central Scotland in the 1930s.

> B
>
> *In the 1930s, most housewives living in tenements had to work very hard in small rooms that required constant tidying and cleaning. Clothes, towels and sheets had to be washed by hand. Work clothes had to be washed and dried nearly every day. Water had to be heated in the wash house boiler shared with other families who lived in the same close. The only alternative for most women was to pay to use the facilities at the public wash house or 'steamie' every week.*

◎ *What evidence is there in Source A to support the view that women's working conditions at home improved between 1930 and 1939?*

What evidence is there in Source B to show that women still had to work hard around the home in the 1930s? (5)

Do not use recalled information.

REMEMBER As a rule, most sources have strengths and weaknesses.

Source A describes improvements such as a washing machine and an electric fire. These new labour-saving devices meant less water being boiled and less time spent cleaning out fireplaces.

Source B mentions working in cramped conditions, constant cleaning and tidying, washing by hand, boiling water in wash houses or going to the 'steamie' once a week.

Some candidates worry about the mini-investigation because the three questions are linked to a common theme and relate to the same sources.

Don't panic! The fact that there is a common theme is an advantage. You know what the three questions are about from the beginning. Also, the examiners will have had some trouble finding two or three sources that can be used to fit the mini-investigation format. As a result, there should be few surprises – you may recognise a source that you have used during the course that has been edited to fit into the mini-investigation format. The most important tip is to remember that each of the questions is asking you to demonstrate different skills. Concentrate on answering each question in the way that you have been shown during the course.

C At Credit level

■ You must identify where the evidence comes from, e.g. in brackets say that it comes from Source A, B or C.

■ Simply writing down the evidence may not be enough – you may have to explain that the evidence suggests or hints that there were other factors.

REMEMBER
At Credit level, if you don't use the sources or recalled information, and if you don't reach a balanced conclusion, you cannot score good marks.

(?) What recalled information, i.e. relevant evidence that is not in the sources, could you use to answer the practice question below?

(?) Consider how to write a balanced conclusion to the question which deals with both sides of the issue, e.g. working conditions improved for some people but not for others. (This is good practice for all candidates but is essential at Credit level.)

◎ Do you think this advert for vacuum cleaners is a reliable source of information about housework in the 1930s? Write an answer and show it to your teacher.

This vacuum cleaner advertisement from the 1930s told housewives to 'just glide the Hoover lightly with the hand. No need to bear down on it. It does all the work itself'.

Practice question

■ How far do you think that working conditions for women at home improved by the 1930s? Use evidence from the sources and your own knowledge to come to a conclusion. (4)

Write one or two paragraphs to answer this question. Allow yourself 10 minutes.

FactZONE

📺 The movement for Women's Suffrage 1890s-1928

1897 National Union of Women's Suffrage Societies (NUWSS) founded. Women's suffrage societies unite behind the leadership of Millicent Fawcett. Supporters of this movement were known as Suffragists, and they set out to educate and form public opinion through meetings, lectures, leaflets etc. Although its leaders were middle class, the NUWSS tried to win the support of working-class women.

1903 Women's Social and Political Union (WSPU) was founded. Mrs Emmeline Pankhurst had grown impatient with the peaceful, law-abiding tactics of the NUWSS. She formed the WSPU with its slogan 'Deeds not words'. Members of the WSPU were known as Suffragettes, and they increasingly became more aggressive in their campaign methods, often ending up in court on charges of breaching the peace, resisting arrest, criminal damage etc.

1906 The Liberals won the General Election and remained in power until 1916. Most Liberal Party leaders opposed granting women the right to vote in parliamentary elections because they believed those women who would qualify to vote would be naturally 'conservative' and would be likely to vote for the opposition. At this time, voting rights were still based on owning or renting property.

1907 Some women broke away from the WSPU to set up the Women's Freedom League.

1908 Suffragette tactics become more militant (i.e. more violent), with Suffragette demonstrations resulting in many women being arrested.

1909 A Conciliation Bill designed to give the vote to female property owners was blocked by the Prime Minister, Asquith. Another Conciliation Bill failed to become law in 1911 and 1912.

1913 Violent Suffragette activity grew until Emily Wilding Davison became a Suffragette martyr when she was killed at the Derby. Suffragette hunger strikers forced the government to introduce the 'Cat and Mouse Act' to prevent women starving themselves to death in prison.

1914 The WSPU abandoned its campaign in order to support the war effort.

1918 The **Representation of the People Act** gave women over 30 the vote, while giving all adult males over 21 the vote. As a result of the different age qualifications, male voters remained in the majority: 13 million men, compared to 8.5 million women, could vote.

1928 The **Representation of the People (Equal Franchise) Act** gave women equal voting rights to men.

Other important legislation

1970 The **Equal Pay Act** said that men and women were to be paid the same wage for doing the same work (this was to come into effect by 1975). An amendment to the Sex Discrimination Act entitled women to equal pay for doing work of the same, similar or equal value.

1975 The **Sex Discrimination Act** said that women were to be treated in the same way as men in education, training, employment and the provision of housing, facilities and services. An amendment to the Act allowed women to work until the age of 65, the same age as men.

28

C **g** To be able to answer questions on content relating to International co-operation and conflict 1790s-1820s, you should know about the following:

- the immediate causes of the Revolutionary War, 1792

- the coalitions formed against France and their degree of success

- the effects of war on civilians in Britain and France, 1792-1805

- the experience of war at sea, 1797-1805

- the Congress of Vienna, 1814-1815

- the Congress System and threats to European peace in the 1820s: Spain and Greece.

f To be able to answer questions on content relating to International co-operation and conflict 1790s-1820s, you should know about the following:

- British views of the French Revolution, 1789-1793

- the Fourth Coalition

- the effects of the war on employment, food supplies and the use of propaganda in Britain

- life on board ship in Nelson's navy

- the treatment of France at the Congress of Vienna, 1814-1815

- the Greek War of Independence, 1822-1829.

The FactZone looks at life on board ship in Nelson's navy.

The practice questions focus on Enquiry Skills at General and Credit levels.

Life aboard ship in Nelson's navy

Battle

In battle, solid round shot was used to penetrate up to a metre of solid oak timbers. The shot would produce plenty of oak splinters creating a large number of casualties. Chain shot was used to rip sails and damage spars, rigging and so on and to restrict the movement of ships under attack. Bar shot was used to bring down masts and disable a ship. Grapeshot was used to kill or maim enemy crews. Marksmen or sharpshooters climbing to high positions in the rigging would shoot at individual officers or men in key positions aboard enemy ships. The aim of an attack was to capture enemy ships, not to sink them. Sails, masts and even crews could be replaced, but a captured enemy ship would mean prize money for the successful crew.

Large battleships had an upper deck, upper gun deck and middle gun deck. Guns were moved into fire out of gun ports, defending the rear or stern of the ship. Aboard a large battleship, the lower gun deck was used as the main living area for the crew. The orlop was the lowest deck where crew would live. Key men such as the ship's surgeon, purser, steward, captains' servant, boatswain and carpenter lived below the waterline. As it was relatively safe from enemy gunfire, the orlop would be the site of an emergency operating theatre during battles.

Daily life

The sailors' day was divided into 'watches'. The ship's bell would be rung every half hour to help the crew to keep track of time and to work out how much of their 'watch' remained. Men slept in hammocks that could be rolled up and stowed in the hammock nettings on the upper deck. These hammock nettings provided some protection from enemy musket balls and oak splinters during battles. The forecastle on the upper deck was the only space aboard a large battleship where sailors could relax when off duty.

Sailors waiting to be punished would be restrained with leg irons. They would be punished on the quarter deck in front of the rest of the crew. They would be beaten (or 'flogged') with a whip known as a 'cat o' nine tails'.

Food

The galley was where food for all of the crew would be prepared. On a large ship, this would mean meals for a crew of about 850 men. Aboard HMS Victory, 580 men at a time sat at 90 tables to eat their meals in 'messes' of four to six men. Breakfast was porridge and a hot drink made from crushed biscuits and hot water known as 'Scotch coffee'. The main meal was a stew of salt beef or pork, or sometimes fish, with oatmeal and boiled peas. Supper consisted of biscuits and butter or cheese. To maintain sailors' health and morale and to prevent scurvy, lime juice was issued. Fresh meat and vegetables were brought aboard as often as possible. However, large ships could carry enough dried and salted food stores to last for six months if necessary.

The quality of food at sea was a serious problem during a long voyage or when on blockade duties. Biscuits became infested with maggots and weevils. Cheese became mouldy and butter became rancid. The quality of salted meat deteriorated. Since the quantity of fresh drinking water was limited, sailors were issued with large quantities of either beer, wine, rum or brandy each day. Sailors were issued with almost 1kg of tobacco per month. Much of this tobacco would be chewed as it helped to reduce the sailors' appetite for food.

Enquiry Skills

European war and peace

Metternich was born in 1773 and served as an Austrian diplomat in Dresden, Berlin and Paris between 1801 and 1809. He became Foreign Minister in 1809 and Chancellor in 1821.

As he had been born abroad and did not move to Vienna until 1794, he was not allowed to control domestic policies and had to focus on foreign affairs. He regarded the period between 1809 and 1815 as the most important of his career - he led Austria into the Fourth Coalition and played a leading role as Austria's delegate to the Congress of Vienna that led to the Treaty of Vienna, 1815. The period 1815-1848 in international relations has been called the period of the 'Metternich System' or 'Congress System'.

Source A is taken from a letter written by Metternich in March 1815.

> **A**
>
> All I ask is for a moral understanding between the great powers whose strength and prestige make them the natural guardians of European destiny.
> I ask that they take no important step, do nothing that might endanger the general European peace, without a previous joint understanding.

◎ 🄖 *How fully does the evidence in Source A explain the role of the great powers in preventing further war in Europe?*
You should use your own knowledge and give reasons for your answer. (4)

❗ **REMEMBER** As part of your revision, list all of the exam-type questions that you have answered in class or for homework and go over how best to approach them.

Answer the question by saying 'how fully' or 'to what extent', e.g. completely, fully, partly, not at all.

Always refer to the source by describing the content in your own words. Don't just write out what the source says – explain its relevance to the question.

In addition, use your own recalled knowledge to say how fully the source contains the information needed to answer the question. Mention any 'gaps' that you can spot in the evidence provided, e.g. the source was written when Austria, Britain, Prussia and Russia signed the Quadruple Alliance.

The 'Final Act' of the Congress of Vienna in June 1815, also known as the Treaty of Vienna, created three new territories: the united kingdom of the Netherlands (Belgium, Holland and Luxembourg), a German Confederation of 39 linked but independent states, and a free city of Cracow (a disputed area of 600 square miles claimed by Russia and Austria).

Two new 'subject' kingdoms were created: Lombardy-Venetia (ruled by the Austrian Emperor) and Poland (ruled by the Russian Tsar). The Swiss Confederation was re-established. The royal families in Spain, Naples, Piedmont, Tuscany and Modena were restored to their former positions of power.

Apart from these and other territorial adjustments, the Congress of Vienna established the system of international diplomacy that survived largely intact until the outbreak of the Great War in 1914.

Source B is from a note sent by Metternich to the Spanish government in December 1822.

Co-operation and conflict

> B
>
> *The Sovereigns of Austria, Prussia, Russia and France were unwilling to meddle in the internal affairs of Spain if her revolution could be kept inside Spanish territory. But this is not the case; this revolution had been the cause of great disasters in other states; it was this revolution which, by its contagious influence and by the intrigues of its leaders created the revolutions of Naples and Piedmont ... The Congress Powers preserved Europe from widespread destruction.*

REMEMBER At Credit level, you should try to give a balanced answer to this type of question by pointing out similarities and differences between the information in the sources.

◎ **C** *To what extent do Sources A and B agree about the aims of the Congress System? (4)*

❓ *Can you use recalled information to point out gaps in the evidence?*

Remember to make clear references to both sources. Remember that both sources were written by Metternich so they will give us a good idea of what he thought about the Congress System. Source B was written seven years after Source A, and much had happened in those years.

Notice that, in Source A, Metternich was giving advice to the great powers, while in Source B Metternich was justifying the action taken by the Congress Powers to the Spanish government. Source B represents the aims of the Congress System being put into action.

Context B: 1890s-1920s

C **g** To be able to answer questions on content relating to International co-operation and conflict 1930s-1945, you should know about the following:

- the Great Powers and their alliances, 1894-1914
- international tension as shown in:
  - the Naval Arms Race, 1906-1914
  - the Balkans, 1908-1913
  - Sarajevo and the outbreak of war
- the experience of war 1914-1918, and its effect on:
- the lives of soldiers on the Western Front
- the lives of civilians in Britain and Germany
- new technology and its effects on the conduct of war on the Western Front, 1914-1918
- the Treaty of Versailles (1919) and the treatment of Germany
- the search for security through the League of Nations, 1919-1928.

f To be able to answer questions on content relating to International co-operation and conflict 1890s-1920s, you should know about the following:

- the two armed camps in Europe, 1900-1914
- the Naval Arms Race, 1906-1914
- the assassination of Archduke Franz Ferdinand at Sarajevo, 1914
- the Home Front in the UK, 1914-1918: employment, food supplies and propaganda
- trench warfare on the Western Front
- the treatment of Germany at Versailles, 1919
- the setting up of the League of Nations.

The FactZones look at trench warfare, new technology, the Home Front and the Paris Peace Conference.

The practice questions focus on Knowledge and Understanding at Credit level and Enquiry Skills at General and Credit levels.

You need to learn these key facts:

Trench warfare

Front-line trenches were usually about seven feet deep and six feet wide. The front of the trench was known as the parapet. At the top of the trench on both sides, sandbags were used to absorb any bullets or shell fragments (shrapnel). It was impossible to see over the top, so there was a ledge, known as a fire-step, to stand on.

Trenches were not dug in straight lines. Both sides knew that the enemy could enter a trench and so must be prevented from shooting straight along it. Therefore, they were dug with alternate fire-bays and traverses creating a zig-zag line. There were wooden duck-boards on the floors of trenches for troops to walk on. Soldiers also made dugouts in the sides of trenches to give them some protection from the weather and shell fire. As the Germans had dug their trench lines first, they were able to take command of higher, and drier, ground. This gave them a clear advantage over their British and French opponents in terms of living conditions and in having stronger defensive positions.

Behind the front-line trenches were support and reserve trenches. Communication trenches linked the trench lines together. Shallow trenches, known as saps, were dug out into no man's land and were used as listening posts and machine gun positions.

Trench life

Living conditions in the trenches were dreadful. Soldiers had to live in the trenches in all weathers. In bad weather, trenches often flooded. Due to the wet conditions and poor hygiene, some soldiers suffered from very painful 'trench foot'.

Daily routine was often very dull. Most days, the soldiers were kept busy:
- cleaning and inspecting weapons and equipment
- removing casualties from the trenches and no man's land
- moving and storing supplies, food rations and equipment
- observing enemy activity
- repairing sand bags and barbed wire defences
- delousing uniforms.

Soldiers had to live with:
- the constant danger of enemy shelling and snipers
- the noise of artillery bombardments
- the death or injury of close friends
- the threat of poison gas attacks
- rats, lice and wasps (in good weather)
- the boring diet of tea, biscuits and tinned beef
- fear of having to go 'over the top'.

You need to learn these key facts:

New technology

Poison gas

Gas could be effective if the wind blew in the right direction and the enemy was taken by surprise. Later in the war, poison gas shells were fired at the enemy. The British army used chlorine and phosgene gases. Phosgene was the more effective poison to use as a tiny amount could kill its victims within a short time. One disadvantage of chlorine gas was that it made the victim cough and this prevented him from breathing in too much poison. The Germans drenched large areas of ground with mustard gas, which caused blisters, to prevent Allied troops from moving into those areas.

Tanks

The British were the first to introduce the armoured vehicle, known as the tank. The sight of the first tanks created panic among the German troops who saw them. Tanks could be effective if the ground was firm enough and there were sufficient troops to hold onto enemy territory captured by the tanks. However, the early tanks were unreliable and too many broke down. It cannot be said that they played a major part in the Allied victory.

Artillery

Artillery caused most of the casualties in trench warfare, e.g. approximately 55% of British casualties compared to 40% caused by machine guns. Large guns increased in quantity and quality as the war went on and new technology made Allied artillery more effective. For example:

- new shells were better at cutting enemy barbed wire
- aircraft flew over enemy trenches taking photographs
- more accurate maps were produced to be used by gunners
- the performance of individual guns was measured and improved
- more than 500 weather stations recorded wind speed, air pressure and temperature as each of them could affect the artillery guns' accuracy.

From the end of 1917, the British used 'hurricane' bombardments lasting only a few hours, restoring the element of surprise to attacks across no man's land, and churning up less of the ground to be covered by advancing infantry or tanks. By this time, British attacks were assisted by smoke shells designed to hide infantry from German machine gunners. The value of heavy artillery increased towards the end of the war and played a major part in the Allied victory in November 1918.

Equally important were the troops of the five Australian and four Canadian divisions who proved to be more than a match for the German defences. These forces from the British Empire transformed the British Army into the driving force behind the Allied victory. Taking full advantage of the new artillery tactics, the British army became the spearhead of the Allied forces, taking on more enemy divisions than the other Allied armies put together. At Amiens in August 1918, the enemy trenches were overwhelmed by the advancing British, and 18 000 Germans were taken prisoner in a single day.

Enquiry Skills

📺 💿 Trench warfare

Source A is a plan of a trench system.

Source B is a trench on the Western Front.

(?) *Are there any important features of trench layout that are not shown in the sources?*

Remember that trench warfare was not new and had been a feature of the American Civil War in the 1860s. On the Western Front, the first trench systems were ready by 1915 with their lines of reserve trenches. By 1916, trench systems were designed to provide defence in depth, with reserve lines stretching back for several miles. The Germans developed the Hindenburg Line in 1917 with its concrete fire positions and machine gun posts, as well as deep underground shelters. However, these German defences were being captured in a single day by 1918, due to new tactics and more effective artillery bombardments. Trench warfare had become obsolete by the end of the war.

❗ REMEMBER Don't just describe what is in the sources, but explain their relevance to the question.

Practice question

C How fully do Sources A and B describe the layout of trench systems on the Western Front?

You should use your own knowledge and give reasons for your answer. **(4)**

Write one or two paragraphs to answer this question. Allow yourself 10 minutes.

You need to know these key facts:

Recruitment

August 1914   At the outbreak of war, thousands of young men rushed to join the army. They were called volunteers. The army promised to keep volunteers from the same area, street or factory in the same regiment, which were known as Pals Regiments. There was massive patriotic propaganda and enthusiasm and many were attracted by the idea of excitement and glory, believing that the war would be over by Christmas.

1914–1915   The First Word War became a war of trenches and attrition on the Western Front. The Government decided to build a large army. The effectiveness of propaganda and the number of volunteers lessened when people heard news about the conditions, the heavy casualties on the Front, and when the likely length of the war became apparent.

January 1916   The Military Service Act – conscription (compulsory military service) was introduced. At first, the law forced all single men aged 18-41 to join up. In 1918 the age was raised to 51.

March 1916   Conscription was extended to all married men. Some categories were exempted: men in reserved occupations (essential jobs, e.g. miners, farmers); men judged unfit; conscientious objectors (people opposed to all war, known as 'conchies'). Tribunals were set up to decide who were genuine conscientious objectors – in 1916, there were over 15 000 'conchies'.

The role of women

Work

The large number of men at war meant new job opportunities for women:
• as nurses or ambulance drivers at the front
• in factories which made the guns, bullets etc. (munitions factories). By 1918 there were over 900 000 'munitionettes'
• in other jobs traditionally done by men (drivers, ticket inspectors etc.)
• in the Women's Land Army, doing farm work
• as secretaries and clerks (500 000).

Politics

When war broke out, most women supported Britain's involvement. Some tried to get men to volunteer by giving white feathers to all young men not in uniform (sometimes, these were soldiers on leave).

Social

Before the war, women were seen as passive and home-centred. War work (e.g. as ambulance drivers and nurses, through which they shared the sufferings on the Front) and the sight of women in uniform led to changes in:
• attitudes towards women and their roles
• fashion for women – it became more comfortable and practical (e.g. trousers)
• social freedoms (e.g. women being able to smoke and visit pubs).

Enquiry Skills

📺 Recruitment

This source shows a British recruiting poster produced during the First World War.

Daddy, what did **YOU** do in the Great War?

◎ **g** *How useful is this poster for studying the British government's methods of encouraging men to volunteer for the armed forces? (5)*

⁇ *Consider what recalled information about recruitment you will need to answer this question properly.*

⁇ *Think about how to create a balanced evaluation, pointing out strengths and weaknesses in the source. This is expected at Credit level, but is a good idea at General level for General/Credit level candidates – posters were only one technique used by the government.*

Mentioning that the source is or isn't a 'primary source' receives no marks at General and Credit levels. Instead, you should mention the date if it is given or give some idea of when you think it was produced.

Always focus your answer on the second part of the question, i.e. government methods of encouraging men to volunteer for the armed forces – in this case, a poster that would be pasted on a wall or notice board.

Notice that the scene in the poster is supposed to represent a time when the war is over, and the young man who didn't volunteer now has a family (and he will have to explain to his children what he did or didn't do in the Great War).

Knowledge and Understanding

📺 💿 The role of women

This source shows a woman bus conductor in London in 1917.

(?) *For the practice question below, think about how large numbers of women became employed in a wide variety of jobs during the First World War.*

(?) *Consider how you could explain why some women issued 'white feathers' to young men.*

Practice question

C Give a brief account of the role women played during the First World War. (4)

Write one or two paragraphs to answer this question. Allow yourself 10 minutes.

You need to learn these key facts:

1914–1918   Britain and France built up tremendous debts to finance the First World War. Large areas of the north of France were devastated.

'The Big Three' were David Lloyd George (British PM), Georges 'Tiger' Clemenceau (French PM) and Woodrow Wilson (US President).

Their aims at the Paris Peace Conference were:

Britain	**France**	**USA**
(wanted **compromise peace**)	(wanted **harsh peace**)	(wanted a **just peace**)
750 000 killed and 1.5 million casualties.	1.4 million killed and 2.5 million casualties. There was massive destruction of land, factories (25 000), railway lines (5 600km) and roads (48 000km).	The USA was not invaded; it suffered only small losses and had no war debts. It entered the war in 1917 as 'a war to end wars'.
The war cost £10 billion (£1 billion borrowed from the USA).		Woodrow Wilson did not fully support Britain and France. He wanted **self-determination** (people ruling themselves) and **international co-operation** (peaceful settling of disputes).
The British people wanted harsh peace and compensation.	The French people wanted Germany to pay **reparations** (compensation) of 200 000 million gold francs to cover damage and war debts.	
Lloyd George feared a harsh treaty would create future bitterness and make Germany too weak to resist communism. Also he wanted to maintain Britain's empire and to begin trading with Germany as soon as possible to help British industry.	Clemenceau wanted Germany to lose much of its land and industry, to greatly reduce its armed forces and to pay France's debts. He wanted to keep Germany weak and unable to attack France again.	**Jan 1918** Fourteen Points were issued by Wilson as a foundation for long-term peace.

The Treaty of Versailles

28 June 1919   The Treaty of Versailles was signed without consulting the new democratic Weimar government in Germany. It was called a Diktat (dictated peace).

The treaty caused certain problems. Many Germans didn't know the war was going badly for them and they felt betrayed by their own politicians who'd signed the **armistice** (cease-fire agreement) and the treaty. In Germany, they became known as the **November Criminals**. There was no self-determination or plebiscite (i.e. a vote by the people on one particular issue) for Germans transferred to Poland, or for German-speakers in Austria and parts of Czechoslovakia.

Enquiry Skills

🔘 ⦿ The 'Big Three' and their aims

Source A is a French poster produced after the First World War (Text says: 'Murderers always return to the scenes of their crime'.)

Source B is an extract from the Allied statement to the German representatives.

> *In the view of the Allied Powers the war which began on August 1 1914 was the greatest crime against humanity and the freedom of peoples that any nation calling itself civilised has ever committed. Germany's responsibility is not confined to having planned and started the war. She is no less responsible for the savage and inhuman manner in which it was conducted. The conduct of Germany is almost unexampled in human history. No less than seven million dead lie buried in Europe because Germany saw fit to go to war. There must be justice for the dead. There must be justice for the people who now stagger under war debts. There must be justice for those millions whose homes and lands the German savagery has spoiled and destroyed.*

⦿ **C** *To what extent do Sources A and B agree about French aims during the peace negotiations of 1919? (4)*

? *Think about what recalled information you can use to point out gaps in the evidence.*

❗ R E M E M B E R
Always remember to answer a question that asks 'to what extent' or 'how fully' with 'partly', 'to some extent' etc.

Make detailed references to both sources. Both sources agree about the death and destruction resulting from the German invasion: Source A mentions 'murderers' and Source B mentions seven million dead. Source A suggests that the French are worried about future German attacks while Source B tries to place blame ('War Guilt') on the Germans, and refers to justice and compensation.

📺 ⊚ The Treaty of Versailles

Source A is a British cartoon about the Treaty of Versailles produced in 1918.

PEACE AND FUTURE CANNON FODDER

The Tiger: "Curious! I seem to hear a child weeping!"

Source B is a British journalist's view in 1929 of the Treaty of Versailles.

> It was a peace of vengeance. It reeked with injustice. It was incapable of fulfilment. It sowed a thousand seeds from which new wars might spring … The absurdity, the wild impossibility, of extracting that vast tribute (reparations) from the defeated enemy … ought to have been obvious to the most ignorant schoolboy …

(?) *When one of the sources is a cartoon, you should be ready to explain what you think the cartoon means. Think about how the titles and words in the cartoons assist us in understanding the cartoonist's point of view, e.g. the children of 1940 will weep because there will be war because of the mistakes made in 1919, and the children of 1940 will be 'cannon fodder', i.e. victims of war.*

(?) *What recalled information can you use to point out gaps in the evidence? For example, there were people in Britain who were keen to punish Germany and didn't believe the terms of the treaty were harsh enough.*

❗ REMEMBER Always try to make clear references to both sources.

Practice question

C How fully do Sources A and B describe British reactions to the terms of the Treaty of Versailles? (5)

Write one or two paragraphs to answer this question. Allow yourself 10 minutes.

Context C: 1930s-1960s

1930s-1945

C **g** To be able to answer questions on content relating to International co-operation and conflict 1930s-1945, you should know about the following:

- the effects of:

  - German rearmament 1933-1939

  - the Czech Crisis 1938

  - the attack on Poland

- the experience of war 1939-1945, and its effect on people's lives in the UK and Germany

- new technology and its effects on the conduct of the war.

f To be able to answer questions on content relating to International co-operation and conflict 1930s-1945, you should know about the following:

- the Czech Crisis, 1938

- aspects of the Home Front in the UK, 1939-1945: civil defence, evacuation, the use of propaganda, air raids

- air warfare.

The FactZones look at:

- the effects of German rearmament, 1933-1938

- the Czech Crisis 1938; the factors behind appeasement

- the attack on Poland, 1939

The practice question focuses on Enquiry Skills at Credit level.

 Effects of German rearmament 1933-1938

1933   Hitler took Germany out of the Disarmament Conference and the League of Nations.

1934   Hitler attempted a forced union (Anschluss) with Austria, breaking the terms of the Treaty of Versailles. Italy, France and the UK joined together to prevent this.

1935   Hitler introduced conscription (compulsory military service), once again breaking the terms of the Treaty of Versailles. Italy, France and the UK formed the Stresa Front to oppose Germany, but the Stresa Front was weakened by the Anglo-German Naval Treaty (allowing the German navy to expand to 35% of the Royal Navy). The Italians invaded Abyssinia (Italy was angry at the limited opposition from the UK and France).

1936   Hitler re-militarised the Rhineland (against the Treaty of Versailles).

The Spanish Civil War broke out. Italy and Germany helped the Nationalist rebels by providing weapons and troops.

Italy and Germany signed the Rome-Berlin Axis (or alliance), breaking up the Stresa Front.

1938   Hitler sent in troops to achieve Anschluss with Austria. 99% of those Austrians who voted in the Nazi-run plebiscite approved the Anschluss.

 The Munich Crisis

1938

Mar   Hitler met Henlein, the Nazi leader of the Sudeten Germans, and ordered him to stir up trouble in the Sudetenland.

May   France and the Soviet Union reaffirmed their support for Czechoslovakia. Hitler finalised his plans to conquer Czechoslovakia for more Lebensraum (living space).

June   Tension and conflict increased in the Sudetenland. The UK and France tried to persuade the Czech government to make concessions to the Sudeten Germans.

Aug   The British Prime Minister was informed that his armed forces were not ready for war.

Sept   Chamberlain met Hitler at Berchtesgaden and they agreed that the Germans could have the Sudetenland. France supported Chamberlain's plan, and together, the UK and France forced the Czech Prime Minister to accept the loss of the Sudetenland.

Chamberlain met Hitler at Bad Godesberg. Hitler made new demands for immediate occupation of the Sudetenland and issued an ultimatum (final threat or demand) to the Czech government.

Chamberlain met Hitler at Munich (with the French and Italian leaders present) and agreed to the immediate transfer of the Sudetenland to Germany.

1939   In March, German troops took over the rest of Czechoslovakia. This was the first territory inhabited largely by non-Germans that Hitler had captured. The German army also seized Memel. This was a former German area that had been occupied by Lithuania since the end of the Great War. It was clear that the agreement made at Munich would not satisfy Hitler's ambitions and Chamberlain moved quickly to guarantee British support for Poland in the event of a German attack.

⦿ Factors behind appeasement

The term 'appeasement' means making concessions to aggressive countries in order to avoid war.
• Without the support of the USA, the British and French were not prepared to take action against aggressive countries.
• Many people in the UK felt that Germany had reasonable grievances against the Treaty of Versailles.
• Chamberlain, the British Prime Minister, like many who had lived through the First World War, was horrified at the possibility of another major war.
• Many people in the UK were against rearmament and supported the League of Nations in the hope that disputes could be settled without countries going to war.
• The British government wanted to protect the British Empire; Canada, Australia, New Zealand and South Africa said that they wouldn't help the UK over petty European disputes.
• The British government feared communism and was not prepared to form an alliance with the Soviet Union against Nazi Germany.
• Appeasement meant postponing the possibility of going to war for as long as possible.

⦿ Attack on Poland 1939

1934   Germany and Poland signed a non-aggression treaty. Fear of Nazi Germany led the Soviet Union to join the League of Nations.

1935   The USSR, France and Czechoslovakia promised 'mutual assistance' if attacked. The Comintern (Communist International) called for a 'popular front' in Europe to combat Fascism (and Nazism).

1936   Hitler was allowed to reoccupy the Rhineland, despite breaking the Treaty of Versailles. The UK and France did not prevent German and Italian involvement in the Spanish Civil War. Germany and Italy signed the Rome-Berlin Axis and, with Japan, the Anti-Comintern Pact. Stalin became suspicious of the British and French policy of appeasing the Germans and Italians.

1938   The German Anschluss with Austria was not opposed, despite this being against the Treaty of Versailles.

1939   The Soviet Union failed to get the UK and France to sign a formal alliance. The UK took several weeks simply to reply. Stalin appointed Molotov as his new Foreign Minister and began secret negotiations with Nazi Germany.

The Soviet Union made a second attempt to ally with the British and French, but the UK and France sent no senior ministers.

The Nazi Foreign Minister, Ribbentrop, went to Moscow. Molotov and Ribbentrop signed a Nazi-Soviet Non-Aggression Pact. This was a promise not to attack each other and it contained a secret protocol (clause or agreement) outlining the division of Poland and Soviet control of the Baltic states.

On 1 September, Germany invaded western Poland. On 3 September, the UK and France declared war on Nazi Germany. The Second World War had begun.

Enquiry Skills

🄅 European crises

Source A was written by Chamberlain before he became the British Prime Minister in 1937.

> War wins nothing, cures nothing, ends nothing. When I think of the 7 million young men who were cut off in the prime, the 13 million who were maimed or mutilated, the misery and suffering of the mothers and the fathers… in war there are no winners, but all are losers.
>
> **A**

Source B is a British cartoon criticising the policy of British appeasement.

❗ **REMEMBER** In a 'How far…' or 'To what extent…' question, always give points of agreement and disagreement.

B

"EUROPE CAN LOOK FORWARD TO A CHRISTMAS OF PEACE", SAYS HITLER

❗ **REMEMBER** Remember that titles and words in cartoons sometimes mean the opposite of what the cartoonist really thinks – for example, Hungary, Poland, Czechoslovakia etc. cannot look forward to a Christmas of peace!

❓ *Think about how you could mention any gaps in either of the sources, e.g. 'Source A says … but Source B makes no reference to this.'*

Practice question

🄒 To what extent do Sources A and B agree about events in Europe in the years 1937–1939? (4)

Write one or two paragraphs to answer this question. Allow yourself 10 minutes.

46

1945-1960s

g **C** To be able to answer questions on content relating to International co-operation and conflict 1945-1960s, you should know about the following:

• the changing influence of the UK, the USA and the USSR after 1945

• the search for security and international co-operation through the United Nations

• threats to world peace:

– the Berlin Crises, 1948-1949 and 1961

– the Cuban Missile Crisis, 1962.

f   To be able to answer questions on content relating to International co-operation and conflict 1945-1960s, you should know about the following:

• the decline of Britain as a world power

• the setting up of the United Nations

• the Cuban Missile Crisis, 1962.

The FactZone looks at the changing influence of the UK, the USA and the USSR, 1945-1952.

The practice questions focus on Enquiry Skills at General and Credit levels.

The changing influence of the UK, USA and USSR, 1945-1952

The origins of the Cold War

The advances made by the Soviet Union's armed forces during 1944 and 1945 meant that huge areas of Eastern Europe were under Stalin's control when the war ended, and he was in no hurry to allow these states to have their independence.

Also, when World War Two ended, the victorious allies had few reasons to remain friends, e.g. the UK and the USA were worried about the spread of communist ideas and Soviet control over large areas of Eastern Europe; the Soviet Union led by Stalin feared the spread of capitalism and democratic ideals.

In 1945, the British leader, Churchill, warned the Americans of the dangers of allowing Europe to be divided between east and west by an 'iron curtain'. In 1946, the American President, Truman, made it clear that the Americans would resist the spread of communism. The Americans were supported by the British, but the growing hostility between West (capitalism) and East (communism) never broke out into full-scale military conflict in Europe. Instead, a 'cold' or undeclared war existed for more than forty years, with one side represented by NATO (West) and the other by the Warsaw Pact (East).

The Marshall Plan, 1947

1946   Churchill made his 'Iron Curtain' speech in the USA as the Soviet Union's control over Eastern Europe continued to grow.

At the Council of Foreign Ministers, the USA blocked all Soviet proposals and condemned their actions in Eastern Europe.

1947   Many parts of Europe suffered economic crisis (e.g. high unemployment) and severe food shortages (bad harvests, 1946). Support for communism was growing in France and Italy.

The UK told the USA that it could no longer afford to support the Greek royalists in their civil war against the communists.

President Truman of the USA announced his intention to contain (or stop) the spread of communism with economic and military aid. This became known as the Truman Doctrine.

The USA announced massive economic aid for Europe under the direction of George Marshall, usually known as Marshall Aid or the Marshall Plan. The plan was to rebuild European economies to halt the spread of communism. This aid was not available to states in Eastern Europe as Stalin ordered East European states not to apply for aid.

1952   The Marshall Plan ended. During its four years, 1947-1951, the USA gave $13 billion, spent according to an Economic Recovery Programme (ERP) drawn up by West European countries in the summer of 1946. Western Europe's economy had much improved by 1952, as had American exports to Europe.

The formation of NATO

1945   The Soviet Union began to establish control over East European satellite (or subordinate) states.

1946   Churchill made his 'Iron Curtain' speech.

1947   Economic crisis in Europe and civil war in Greece led to the Truman Doctrine and Marshall Plan to halt the spread of communism.

The UK and the USA merged their zones in occupied Germany (known as Bizonia).

The Soviet Union set up Cominform to increase its control over Eastern Europe.

1948   Communists took control of Czechoslovakia.

West European countries formed the Brussels Treaty Organisation (BTO).

France merged its zone in Germany with Bizonia to form Trizonia.

A new currency, the Deutschmark, was introduced.

The Soviet authorities began the Berlin blockade, fearing the revival of German strength. The western allies responded with the Berlin Airlift.

1949   The BTO became the North Atlantic Treaty Organisation (NATO) with the USA and Canada as new members, and the USA as the strongest partner.

THE TRANSATLANTIC UMBRELLA

"There seems to be a constitutional objection to opening it right out."

◎ *Do you think that this cartoonist is making an accurate comment on the role of the USA in the formation of NATO? Write down your answer and show it to your teacher.*

The man (Uncle Sam) with the umbrella represents the USA and the children are European states seeking his protection.

48

 # Knowledge and Understanding

The Berlin airlift

The source is about the Berlin airlift, 1948.

> *At the end of World War Two, Berlin was divided into a western sector controlled by the USA and its western allies, and an eastern sector controlled by the Soviet Union. The two sides disagreed about the future of Germany. Stalin, the Soviet leader hoped to force the western powers out of Berlin, as it was deep inside the Soviet zone of occupied Germany.*

◉ ⓖ *Explain why Stalin blockaded Berlin in 1948. (3)*

To answer this question, you should give at least three reasons why Stalin forced the Berlin airlift. One of these reasons must be from recall.

From the source:
Stalin hoped to force the western powers out of Berlin; the Soviet Union and the western powers disagreed about the future of occupied Germany and divided Berlin; Stalin was against the idea of the western powers having influence deep inside the Soviet zone of occupied Germany.

From recall:
The Soviet Union wanted to keep Germany weak and divided; the Soviet Union was against the western allies building up the economic strength of the zones that they occupied; Stalin thought that he could take advantage of the fact that all road and rail links to Berlin went through the Soviet zone of occupation; Stalin was reacting to the fact that the western allies were working to prevent the spread of communist influence in western Europe.

! REMEMBER As part of your revision, list all of the exam-type questions that you have answered in class or for homework and go over how best to approach them.

Suggested answer

> Stalin blockaded Berlin in 1948 because he wanted to force the western allies out of Berlin. It was deep inside the German territory occupied by the Soviet Union. Stalin thought that he could take advantage of the fact that all road and rail links to Berlin went through Soviet-controlled territory. At the same time, the Soviet Union disagreed with the western allies about the future of occupied Germany. Stalin wanted Germany to be weak and divided.

The Marshall Plan

— Спасибо высоким господам, поддерживают меня, старуху, кто чем может!

Source A is a Soviet cartoon attacking the Marshall Plan of 1947, claiming that it is an attempt at US world domination.

◎ *9 What was the Soviet Union's opinion of the Marshall Plan as shown in Source A? (4)*

Always describe the point of view or attitude revealed in the source, e.g. it is hostile to the Marshall Plan. It is a good idea to quote from the source to provide evidence for your statement of attitude, e.g. Europe, weakened by war and destruction (the image of Death and the damaged helmet), was likely to become dependent on American aid.

Use your knowledge of the topic to explain why the Soviet Union had this point of view, e.g. the Marshall Plan went hand in hand with the political and military power of the USA (and then NATO); the Marshall Plan was one element of a programme designed to prevent Communist or Soviet domination of Europe.

The formation of NATO

Source B is the view of the Soviet government on the establishment of NATO in 1949.

> **B**
>
> *The North Atlantic Treaty has nothing in common with the aims of self-defence of the states, who are threatened by no-one and whom no-one intends to attack. On the contrary, the Treaty has an aggressive characteristic and is aimed against the USSR.*

! **R E M E M B E R** Always describe the point of view or attitude revealed in the source.

(?) *For the first practice question, think about how you can use your knowledge of the topic to explain why the Soviet Union had this point of view.*

(?) *Use recalled knowledge to say how fully the source contains the information needed to answer the question. Mention any 'gaps' that you can spot in the evidence provided, e.g. important events or developments not mentioned in the source.*

! **R E M E M B E R** You do not have to remember exact dates for every topic but it is very useful to be able to put key events into the order in which they took place.

Practice questions

g 1 How fully does the evidence in Source B explain why the Soviet Union opposed the establishment of NATO?

You should use your own knowledge and give reasons for your answer. (4)

c 2 Discuss the Soviet government's attitude towards the establishment of NATO in 1949. (5)

Write one or two paragraphs to answer each question, allowing 10 minutes per question.

g C To be able to answer questions on content relating to the USA 1850-1880, you should know about the following:

- Manifest Destiny and westward expansion:
  - federal policy: effects on Indians (native Americans)
  - relations between slave and non-slave states

- the rise of the Republican Party in the 1850s

- Abraham Lincoln as President and his idea of the Union

- slavery as a cause of the Civil War

- Southern secession and the outbreak of the Civil War

- Reconstruction, 1865-1878, as seen in:
  - the introduction of Negro or African Americans' rights
  - the Freedman's Bureau
  - the activities of carpetbaggers

- reaction in the South to post-war reconstruction

- treatment of the Negroes or African Americans as seen in the rise of the Ku Klux Klan and the Black Codes

- Indian opposition to westward expansion and to federal policy towards westward expansion.

f To be able to answer questions on content relating to the USA 1850-1880, you should know about the following:

- wagon trains, railroads and westward expansion

- the effects of westward expansion by prospectors and Mormons

- the movement of the Plains Indians (particularly the Sioux) to reservations

- attitudes to Negro or African American slavery

- Negro or African American life on plantations in the South

- Abraham Lincoln and his idea of the Union

- the attack on Fort Sumter and the outbreak of the Civil War

- Negro or African American slavery in the South, 1865-1878

- the Ku Klux Klan

- the Sioux revolt in the 1870s.

The FactZones deal with slavery and the outbreak of the Civil War.

The practice questions focus on Knowledge and Understanding at General and Credit levels and Enquiry Skills at Credit level.

📺 Background to slavery

■ By the second half of the eighteenth century, slavery existed in all thirteen colonies and was very important for the economic prosperity of the southern colonies.

■ The spread of cotton production after the invention of the cotton gin in 1793 sharply increased the demand for slave labour and made possible the creation of large plantations or farms worked by small armies of slaves in the South. The demand for raw cotton in the North and in Europe made cotton the nation's most valuable crop, as it accounted for 50-60% of the USA's total exports by the 1850s.

■ Slavery became the South's 'peculiar institution', as slavery had never been as important in the North. In 1861, the population of the South included nearly four million slaves.

Life on a plantation in the South

■ Slaves in the South worked as skilled craftsmen, nurses, mule drivers and mill workers, as well as field hands (or labourers) and house servants.

■ Slave ownership varied according to size, location and crops grown; slaves produced most of the cotton crop, as well as tobacco, rice and sugar. By the 1850s, slaves made up about one-third of the population in the South. 75% of farms and plantations employed less than fifty slaves.

■ Slave owners looked upon slavery as an investment as well as a method of controlling the growing African American population. Some slave owners treated their slaves quite well, but many subjected their slaves to countless rules and regulations and harsh discipline. They often broke up slave families.

■ Slaves often tried to run away, and some attacked their owners and overseers (white foremen who looked after the slaves for the owner); runaway slaves were often beaten, and sometimes maimed to discourage further escapes. Although most slaves had their own living quarters or cabins, their standard of living was far below that of most people living in the USA, and they had little or no freedom to travel or visit family or friends owned by other slave owners. Nearly all slaves were baptised Christians but they did not worship beside their Christian slave owners. Many female slaves had children whose fathers were slave owners or overseers; these children were slaves, like their mothers.

Anti-slavery

You should remember that slavery persisted in countries other than the USA. The British had freed all slaves living in their Empire in 1883, but Brazil did not free all of its slaves until 1888. The international slave trade, the transportation of slaves from one country to another, had ended by 1820 and this forced American slave owners to rely on slaves born in the USA. To justify their use of slaves, slave owners tried to claim that slavery was necessary, both to provide a cheap workforce and to control the large population of non-white slaves living in the USA.

William Lloyd Garrison began an anti-slavery campaign in Boston in 1831. The Anti-Slavery Society was established in 1833. Harriet Beecher Stowe's anti-slavery novel, 'Uncle Tom's Cabin', was published in 1852 and became a key piece of anti-slavery propaganda.

People and power

Knowledge and Understanding

⊞ Slavery and the American Civil War

> **REMEMBER**
> A conclusion is not always necessary in an 8-mark answer, but it is advisable to write one for questions that ask you to explain or comment on how important a person or event was.

◎ ⒢ *How important was slavery as a cause of the American Civil War? (8)*

(Note: for this answer you should write a short essay of several paragraphs.)

■ This type of Credit level question expects you to write a short essay of two or three paragraphs. It should take about ten to fifteen minutes to write.

■ You should try to identify and explain five or six reasons why the American Civil War broke out, including slavery.

■ You are expected to say how important you think slavery was as a cause of the Civil War, e.g. very important or quite important.

■ End your short essay with a brief, but balanced conclusion.

■ Look at the FactZones on pages 53, 56 and 57 and study the timeline of events leading up to the outbreak of the Civil War.

■ The key point is that slavery was an important cause of the civil war, but not the only one.

Fort Sumter under attack.

English
Mon-Fri 0200-0400
Sat-Sun 0300-0500

English 1: Macbeth
29 Mar '99   Sun night/Mon morning 0200-0400
2 May '99   Sat night/Sun morning 0300-0500 rpt

English 2: Poetry
30 Mar '99   Mon night/Tues morning 0200-0400
8 May '99   Fri night/Sat morning 0300-0500 rpt

English 3: Reading & Writing non-fiction Texts
31 Mar '99   Tues night/Wed morning 0200-0400
9 May '99   Sat night/Sun morning 0300-0500 rpt

Maths
Mon-Fri 0200-0400
Sat-Sun 0300-0500

Maths 1
1 Apr '99   Wed night/Thurs morning 0200-0400
29 May '99   Fri night/Sat morning 0300-0500 rpt

Maths 2
2 Apr '99   Thurs night/Fri morning 0200-0400
30 May '99   Sat night/Sun morning 0300-0500 rpt

Maths 3
3 Apr '99   Fri night/Sat morning 0300-0500
5 Jun '99   Fri night/Sat morning 0300-0500 rpt

Science
Mon-Fri 0200-0400
Sat-Sun 0300-0500

Science 1: Physics
4 Apr '99   Sat night/Sun morning 0300-0500
15 May '99   Fri night/Sat morning 0300-0500 rpt

Science 2: Animal Biology
5 Apr '99   Sun night/Mon morning 0200-0400
16 May '99   Sat night/Sun morning 0300-0500 rpt

Science 3: Chemistry
6 Apr '99   Mon night/Tues morning 0200-0400
22 May '99   Fri night/Sat morning 0300-0500 rpt

Science 4: Plant Biology
7 Apr '99   Tues night/Wed morning 0200-0400
23 May '99   Sat night/Sun morning 0300-0500 rpt

French
Mon-Fri 0200-0400
Sat-Sun 0300-0500

French 1
6 Mar '99   Fri night/Sat morning 0300-0500
9 Apr '99   Thurs night/Fri morning 0200-0400 rpt

French 2
7 Mar '99   Sat night/Sun morning 0300-0500
10 Apr '99   Fri night/Sat morning 0300-0500 rpt

German
Mon-Fri 0200-0400
Sat-Sun 0300-0500

14 Mar '99   Sat night/Sun morning 0300-0500
8 Apr '99   Wed night/Thurs morning 0200-0400 rpt

Spanish
Mon-Fri 0200-0400
Sat-Sun 0300-0500

13 Mar '99   Fri night/Sat morning 0300-0500
11 Apr '99   Sat night/Sun morning 0300-0500 rpt
1 May '99   Fri night/Sat morning 0300-0500 rpt

Geography
Mon-Fri 0200-0400
Sat-Sun 0300-0500

Geography 1: Human Geography
21 Mar '99   Sat night/Sun morning 0300-0500
12 Apr '99   Sun night/Mon morning 0200-0400 rpt

Geography 2: Physical Geography
27 Mar '99   Fri night/Sat morning 0300-0500
13 Apr '99   Mon night/Tues morning 0200-0400 rpt

Geography 3: Development, Population and Environment Issues
27 Feb '99   Fri night/Sat morning 0300-0500
28 Mar '99   Sat night/Sun morning 0300-0500 rpt
14 Apr '99   Tues night/Wed morning 0200-0400 rpt

All BITESIZE programmes will be shown over the Easter hoidays

 **DON'T FORGET TO SET YOUR VIDEO THE NIGHT BEFORE!**

transmission dates continued

History

Mon-Fri 0200-0400
Sat-Sun 0300-0500

History 1: Modern European and World History
15 Apr '99 Wed night/Thurs morning 0200-0400
6 Jun '99 Sat night/Sun morning 0300-0500 rpt

History 2: Schools History Project
16 Apr '99 Thurs night/Fri morning 0200-0400
12 Jun '99 Fri night/Sat morning 0300-0500 rpt

Business Studies

Mon-Fri 0200-0400
Sat-Sun 0300-0500

28 Feb '99 Sat night/Sun morning 0300-0500
25 Apr '99 Sat night/Sun morning 0300-0500 rpt
19 Jun '99 Fri night/Sat morning 0300-0500 rpt

Design and Technology

Mon-Fri 0200-0400
Sat-Sun 0300-0500

Design and Technology 1
17 Apr '99 Fri night/Sat morning 0300-0500

Design and Technology 2
18 Apr '99 Sat night/Sun morning 0300-0500

Religious Education

Mon-Fri 0200-0400
Sat-Sun 0300-0500

Religious Education
20 Mar '99 Fri night/Sat morning 0300-0500
24 Apr '99 Fri night/Sat morning 0300-0500 rpt
13 Jun '99 Sat night/Sun morning 0300-0500 rpt

Standard Grade Bitesize

Standard Grade English

Mon-Fri 0200-0400
Sat-Sun 0300-0500

29 Mar '99 Sun night/Mon morning 0200-0400
15 Apr '99 Wed night/Thurs morning 0200-0400 rpt

Standard Grade Maths

Mon-Fri 0200-0400
Sat-Sun 0300-0500

21 Mar '99 Sat night/Sun morning 0300-0500
12 Apr '99 Sun night/Mon morning 0200-0400 rpt

Standard Grade French

Mon-Fri 0200-0400
Sat-Sun 0300-0500

28 Mar '99 Sat night/Sun morning 0300-0500
14 Apr '99 Tues night/Wed morning 0200-0400 rpt

Standard Grade Geography

Mon-Fri 0200-0400
Sat-Sun 0300-0500

27 Mar '99 Fri night/Sat morning 0300-0500
13 Apr '99 Mon night/Tues morning 0200-0400 rpt

For more information about **BITESIZE**
check out:

(Ceefax)   page 633 (BBC2)
(Web Site)   www.bbc.co.uk/education/revision
(Telephone)   0181 746 1111

BITESIZE Revision Books can be ordered by phoning 019375 41001 (9am–4pm Mon–Fri) and are available from all good bookshop

All BITESIZE programmes will be shown over the Easter hoidays

 ***DON'T FORGET TO SET YOUR VIDEO THE NIGHT BEFORE!***

Suggested answer

The American Civil War broke out for a number of reasons. There were deep political and economic differences between the North and South. The South had come to depend on slave labour to grow cotton, tobacco and rice crops, as well as to do many other jobs both on plantations and in everyday life. People in the South feared that ending slavery would ruin them financially and create huge social problems once the slaves were set free. Abolitionists in the North believed that slavery was evil and should be ended.

As the USA grew and new territories in the West were settled, people in the North and South wanted to move there. The 1850 Compromise tried to balance the number of slave and free states in the US Senate, but the Fugitive Slave Law gave greater rights to owners of runaway slaves. Tension between slave owners and abolitionists grew. In 1854, violence erupted in the states of Kansas and Nebraska. In 1857, the Dred Scott Case appeared to extend the rights of slave owners into the free states. In 1859, the abolitionist John Brown tried to lead a slave revolt in Virginia. Abraham Lincoln was elected President of the USA in 1860, and people in the South feared that he would try to abolish slavery.

States in the South tried to secede from the Union in order to protect their right to own slaves. However, President Lincoln was not prepared to allow them to set up a Confederate States of America. The Civil War was won by those who wanted to preserve the Union. When the North won the Civil War, slavery was abolished in all states, whether they supported the Union or not.

In conclusion, the existence of slavery in the South and the rights of slave owners were two of the key factors leading to the outbreak of the Civil War. Most of the other factors were linked to slavery in one way or another. Therefore, slavery was the most important cause of the Civil War.

This answer would receive eight marks.

! REMEMBER Make sure that you answer exactly what the question asks – don't make the mistake of writing about a similar topic.

! REMEMBER When you are asked a question, remember that there is usually more than one possible answer.

55

People and power

📺 Attitudes towards slavery

■ Many people in the North were abolitionists (against slavery) because they believed that it was cruel and inhuman to own other people. Some abolitionists were against slavery because of the harm that it did to white people in the South: slavery encouraged cruelty to other humans; slave owners often raped and abused their slaves; poor whites who did not own land or slaves found it difficult to find work and became lazy or turned to crime etc.

■ Anti-abolitionists in the North feared the results of granting African Americans their freedom, e.g. political equality for the growing population of African Americans. Some abolitionists supported the idea of purchasing land in Africa and setting up colonies of former slaves in West Africa (rather than encourage former slaves to become citizens of the USA).

■ Many people in the North opposed the spread of slavery into the West, and this turned into a political struggle between states in the North and South. Many people in the South feared that the North would forbid slavery in the West. As the USA expanded into the West, people in slave-owning and free states became concerned at the shift in the balance of power between North and South, e.g. would slave-owning states outnumber the free states where there were no slaves?

■ There has been much debate about Abraham Lincoln's views on whether or not slavery should be abolished. He was born in a slave state and recent biographers have claimed that he was known to have used the offensive language of his own time to describe non-whites. Also, he is reported to have made offensive remarks about slaves. He openly criticised the 'peculiar institution' of slavery, but he could not see a way to abolish slavery in the USA. In 1862, during the Civil War, Lincoln said that his chief objective was to 'save the Union, and not to save or to destroy slavery'.

A slave auction in Virginia, USA, 1861.

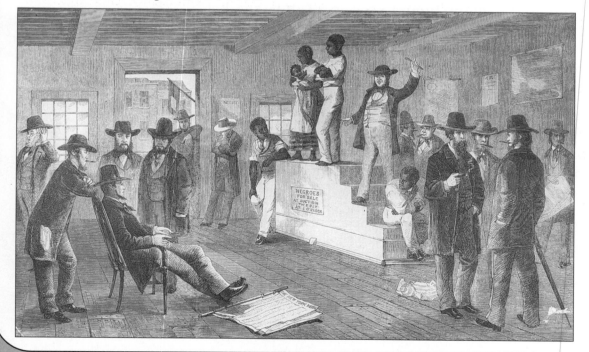

Timeline: slavery and the outbreak of the Civil War

1820 The 1820 Compromise tried to balance the number of slave-owning and free states by preventing the spread of slavery beyond the 36/30 line drawn on maps of the USA to show that territory north of this line should not have slaves. At the same time, the slave state of Missouri was allowed to join the USA in 1820 (a non-slave or free state called Maine was allowed to join at the same time). These agreements were also known as the Missouri Compromise and put off discussion about the spread of slavery into new territory in the West for many years.

1850 The 1850 Compromise tried to solve the problem of allowing California to enter the Union, by allowing California to become a free state, so long as stricter laws were passed to make it easier to return escaped slaves to their owners.

1854 The Kansas-Nebraska Act tried to allow both states to join the Union so long as both held a referendum to decide whether either would be a slave-owning or a free state. This compromise led to violence and bloodshed over the whole issue of the spread of slavery into the West.

1857 The Supreme Court's decision on the Dred Scott Case stated that as a former slave was not a citizen of the United States, this man had no rights, so must remain a slave and be returned to his master. Also, the free state where Dred Scott lived had no right to deprive the man who had owned Dred Scott of his property (i.e. Dred Scott!). This decision pleased the supporters of slavery and horrified the abolitionists.

1858 Abraham Lincoln gave his famous 'House Divided' speech.

1859 John Brown and his abolitionist followers attacked a government ammunition store at Harper's Ferry in Virginia, a slave-owning state. Brown hoped to start a slave revolt against the slave owners in Virginia. Brown was captured and executed for treason. He became a hero of the abolitionists.

1860 In November, Abraham Lincoln won the presidential election with only 40% of the votes. In December, South Carolina seceded or resigned from the Union.

1861

Jan–Feb Mississippi, Florida, Alabama, Georgia, Louisiana and Texas seceded from the Union.

March Lincoln was inaugurated as President.

April Union troops based at Fort Sumter, South Carolina, are attacked by rebel forces (also known as Confederates) and the Civil War begins between those loyal to the Union and those who claimed that individual states had the right to leave the Union.

June The military campaigns began. Lincoln and his Union forces had major advantages: double the population of the Confederate states; a navy to blockade Confederate ports; factories to supply vast quantities of weapons and equipment. The ruthless tactics of the Union commanders, Grant and Sherman, wore down the Confederates.

People and power

Abraham Lincoln and slavery

Source A is from 'Abraham Lincoln' by Norman Kolpas.

> *Lincoln addressed the South directly by saying that although the Republicans thought that slavery was wrong, they would not risk destroying the Union by trying to stamp it out. However, he stressed that he would not stand for the spread of Southern slavery into any new territories saying: 'Thinking slavery wrong, as we do, we cannot yield to slave owners.'*

A

◎ **g** *What was Lincoln's attitude towards slavery? (4)*

To answer this question, you need to identify at least three main points in the source, such as:

■ the Republicans thought that slavery was wrong (and Lincoln was a Republican)

■ the Union was in danger if slavery was attacked, so the Republicans would not try to stamp out slavery in the South

■ Lincoln opposed slavery spreading into any new territories

■ the Republicans would not give in to the slave owners and allow them to take slaves into the new territories.

You also need to mention one piece of relevant recalled information such as:

■ the 1820 Compromise had tried to balance the number of slave-owning and free states by preventing the spread of slavery into territory north of the 36/30 line, but it had not solved the question of territory west of the slave-owning states in the South

■ Abraham Lincoln gave his famous 'House Divided' speech in 1858, when he attacked the institution of slavery, although he admitted that he saw no means of ending it.

Suggested answer

Abraham Lincoln was a Republican so he thought that slavery was wrong. In his famous 'House Divided' speech, he had criticised the institution of slavery. He thought that the Union was in danger if slavery in the South was attacked. At the same time, he opposed the spread of slavery into any of the new territories. Lincoln and the Republicans were not prepared to allow slave owners to take slaves into the new territories.

The sentence in **bold** represents recalled information.

This answer would be awarded four marks.

How useful is this picture as evidence of Lincoln's role in setting American slaves free? Show your answer to this question to your teacher.

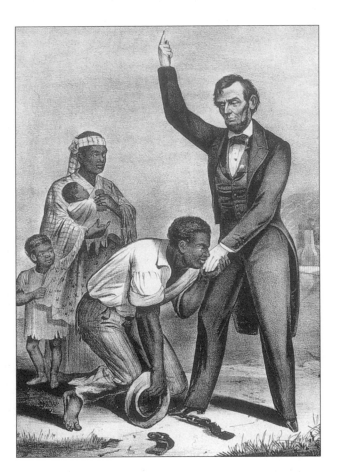

Lincoln proclaimed the emancipation (setting free) of American slaves in January 1863.

People and power

Practice question

C Describe the events that led to the setting up of the Confederacy, between November 1860 and February 1861. (4)

Write one or two paragraphs to answer this question. Allow yourself 10 minutes.

Enquiry Skills

Attitudes towards slavery

Source B was written by Orville Browning who was a Republican and a close friend of Lincoln.

! REMEMBER
If the question refers to a source, make clear references to the source in your answer.

> **B**
>
> *I believe that slavery is the sole, original cause of the present unhappy condition of affairs. A large majority of the people in the free states of this Union believe as I do; and so believing, many of them, good and patriotic people, are anxious that war shall be made the occasion of wiping out slavery.*

! REMEMBER
When you say when the source was written, be precise and give a date rather than saying 'at the time'.

◎ **ⓒ** *How useful is Source B as evidence of American attitudes towards slavery? (4)*

Remember that to answer this Credit level question, you should think about:

■ who wrote the source and why this is important when deciding whether or not the source is useful

■ what the source tells us, and whether or not this information is useful

■ when the source was written, and whether this makes the source more or less useful

■ why the source was written and whether or not this is significant

■ summing up your answer – you can state your conclusion about the source at the beginning of your answer

■ writing a balanced answer, i.e. the source is useful for several reasons, but it has its weaknesses as well.

Suggested answer

This source is quite useful because it was written by a Republican, and a close friend of Lincoln. Republicans were against the spread of slavery into the new territories.

The author suggests that many people in the free states were prepared to go to war to end slavery in the South. There is no date given to tell us when the source was written. Therefore, we do not know whether or not the author's views were shared by many people in the free states at the time when the source was written.

The author of the source could be exaggerating when he says that a large majority of people in the free states supported going to war to end slavery. There were people in the free states who believed that attacking slavery in the South could destroy the Union.

This answer would be awarded 4 marks.

Plan a balanced evaluation pointing out strengths and weaknesses in the source.

In the exam, remember:

REMEMBER Mention the date of the source, if it is given, or give some idea of when you think the source was produced, but don't write 'at the time'.

61

REMEMBER Mentioning that the source is or isn't primary receives no marks at General or Credit level.

At Foundation level
There will be about 14-15 questions to answer.

The questions will be worth 2, 3 or 4 marks and all of them are source-based.

You write your answers in the exam booklet, in the spaces provided.

The answer space will give you a clue as to how long your answer should be, and how many points or reasons you should give.

At General level
There will be about 14 questions to answer.

Most questions are worth 3 or 4 marks; there may be a 5-mark Enquiry Skills question in Unit I.

The marks for each question will give you a clue as to how detailed your answer should be.

All questions are source-based. Some Enquiry Skills questions expect you to use recalled information in your answer (the wording of the question will make it clear).

At Credit level
There should be 13 or 14 questions to answer.

Most questions at Credit level are worth 4, 5 or 6 marks.

As at General level, some Enquiry Skills questions expect you to use recalled information in your answer (the wording of the question will make it clear).

All Knowledge and Understanding answers must be based on recalled knowledge.

People and power

g C To be able to answer questions on content relating to India 1917-1947, you should know about the following:

- the influence of the British Raj on the government of India, including education, communications, trade and the development of democracy

- the changing attitudes of the British towards Indian self-government

- discontent in India arising from:
  - economic exploitation
  - political and social discrimination
  - religious and social divisions amongst Indians

- Gandhi's non-violent opposition to British rule, 1917-1941

- resistance leading to violence: Amritsar

- Indian rejection of British initiatives:
  - Simon Commission
  - Cripps Mission

- support for the Congress Party and the Muslim League

- Muslim direct action and the roles of Jinnah and Nehru

- Indian independence and partition.

f To be able to answer questions on content relating to India 1917-1947, you should know about the following:

- the Raj and the government of India

- the development and use of railways

- the Salt Tax

- the caste system

- Gandhi's tactics

- the Amritsar Massacre, 1919

- Muslim direct action, 1946-1947

- Indian independence and partition; the role of Lord Mountbatten.

The practice questions focus on Knowledge and Understanding at Credit level and Enquiry Skills at General and Credit levels.

Knowledge and Understanding

The British Raj

◎ Ⓖ *Describe how the British Raj affected the lives of the Indian population. (8)*
(Note: for this answer you should write a short essay of several paragraphs.)

■ This type of Credit level question expects you to write a short essay of two or three paragraphs. It should take you about ten to fifteen minutes to write your essay. This type of short essay question can appear in Unit I, II or III of the exam.

■ In this example, you are expected to identify and describe, in detail, five or six important effects that the British Raj had on the Indian population, e.g. in areas such as education and communications; trade and economic exploitation; political and social discrimination; violent and non-violent opposition to British rule.

■ It is a good idea to practise writing short essay answers on topics from Units I, II and III as part of your revision.

The Viceroy of India being carried in a rickshaw by Indian servants, 1939.

⑦ *What does this photograph tell us about British attitudes towards Indians during the Raj? Discuss your response to this question with your teacher.*

People and power

Evaluating sources

Source A is a description of the events at Dandi in 1930 written by an American journalist.

> *They marched steadily with heads up, without the encouragement of music or cheering or any possibility that they might escape serious injury or death. The police rushed out and methodically and mechanically beat down the second column. There was no fight, no struggle, the marchers simply walked forward until struck down. There was no shouting, only groans after they fell. Not one of the marchers raised an arm to fend off the blows.*

A

REMEMBER
All sources are useful, even when they are biased and unreliable.

◎ ❾ *How useful is Source A as evidence of non-violent opposition to British rule? (4)*

You can begin your answer to the question by writing something like 'This source is quite useful because ... '

Relate your answer to the second half of the question by discussing the evidence of non-violent protest. Identify points such as: there was no fighting back on the part of demonstrators; there was no shouting or music; demonstrators did not fend off blows from the police.

The eyewitness was an American journalist rather than an Indian or someone from Britain, so the author's point of view may be more likely to be unbiased. Mention the fact that the source can only tell us so much about what happened as it represents only one point of view.

Comparing sources

You could be asked to compare the evidence in more than one source, e.g. where they agree or disagree and the evidence or reasons for this, or the usefulness or value of two sources.

Here is a second source about the events at Dandi in 1930.

Source B gives the views of an Indian on the events at Dandi.

> England is no longer regarded as the champion of fair dealing and high principles. Instead, England is seen as the upholder of racial supremacy and the exploiter of those outside its borders. Asia can now afford to look down on Europe, where before she looked up.

◎ **ⓒ** *To what extent do Sources A and B agree about the non-violent demonstration at Dandi? (4)*

Remember that Source A contains a description, while Source B contains someone's opinion. The person who wrote Source B was an Indian and they may be biased. Notice that Source A points out the dignity and bravery of the Indian demonstrators, while Source B notes that Asians can look down on the English (i.e. British) after what they did at Dandi.

In both sources, there is a clear divide between Indians and the British: in Source A, the authorities are brutal while the Indians are incredibly brave. In Source B, the British authorities are accused of believing in the racial supremacy of Europeans and being determined to exploit Asians.

A key point from recall is how much opposition to British rule grew after 1930.

❓ *Use recalled knowledge to decide the extent to which Sources A and B contain the information required to answer the practice question below: in this case, were the attacks on the non-violent demonstrators widely publicised; was the opinion of Source B's author shared by many Indians?*

❓ *Did support for non-violent demonstrations grow or decline after the events at Dandi?*

❗ REMEMBER
At Credit level, you should try to give a balanced answer to a question by pointing out both the similarities and differences between the information in each of the sources, e.g. one source may contain more information, or one may not be as reliable as another.

People and power

Practice question

ⓖ How fully do Sources A and B explain the growth of opposition to British rule in India in the 1930s?

You should use your own knowledge and give reasons for your answer. (4)

Write one or two paragraphs to answer this question. Allow yourself 10 minutes.

Russia 1914-1917

g **C** To be able to answer questions on content relating to Russia 1914-1917, you should know about the following:

- the nature of Tsarist government
- discontent under the Tsar arising from:
    - economic hardship (on the land; in the factories)
    - political opposition (liberals, Social Revolutionaries, Social Democrats etc.)
    - effects of the First World War (casualties at the front; food and fuel shortages at home)
- the February/March Revolution 1917
- the formation and characteristics of the Provisional Government
- discontent under the Provisional Government arising from
    - continuation of the war
    - failure to solve economic and social problems
- the October/November Revolution 1917.

f To be able to answer questions on content relating to Russia 1914-1917, you should know about the following:

- the effects of the First World War on Russian civilians
- the abdication of Tsar Nicholas II
- demands for 'Peace, bread and land!'
- the seizure of power by the Bolsheviks in October/November 1917

As you revise this topic, you may have come across books that refer to the February (or March) Revolution, and the October (or November) Revolution. What dates should you use?

It doesn't matter. The confusing dates are the result of Russia using a different calendar from the rest of Western Europe and North America in 1917. The February Revolution, according to the Russian calendar, is the March Revolution according to our calendar (as well as the modern Russian calendar!). You will never lose a mark by referring to one or other calendar, as each is correct, in its own way.

The FactZone deals with discontent under the Provisional Government, 1917.

66

Discontent under the Provisional Government, 1917

The soviets

The soviets or councils were made up of soldiers, sailors or workers in Russian towns and cities. They were set up after the February/March Revolution to make sure that food, fuel and other supplies were rationed or shared out equally, at a time when people could not trust government officials to do this job. At the same time, they gave ordinary people a chance to run their own area. This was something that they had not been allowed to do when the Tsar was in power.

After a short time, they became the local council or government in an area, and the leaders of each soviet had a great deal of power, e.g. in Russia's capital city, Petrograd, the soviet became as important as the Provisional Government. During 1917, so many soviets or councils were set up that they decided to organise a meeting or congress of soviets from all over Russia to discuss important national issues that affected all of them. It was clear that the Provisional Government could not claim to be the only government in Russia.

Problems facing the Provisional Government

In September 1917, the Provisional Government faced several serious problems:

■ the workers and peasants were very unhappy at how little their lives had improved since the February/March Revolution

■ Russia remained at war and the German victories continued

■ the Petrograd and Moscow soviets were growing more powerful and were not happy with the policies of the Provisional Government

■ the Provisional Government needed support from Bolsheviks in Petrograd to defeat Kornilov's attempt to seize power

■ Lenin and the Bolsheviks were gaining more supporters in the soviets

■ Lenin and the Bolsheviks were plotting to overthrow the Provisional Government.

The October/November Revolution 1917

Lenin was leader of the Bolsheviks when they seized power from the Provisional Government in Petrograd. As Lenin was hiding from the Provisional Government (he had been accused of being a German spy), Lenin sent secret instructions for his supporters to prepare to seize power (shortly before the Bolsheviks took action, Lenin returned to Petrograd in disguise to take control of planning).

Trotsky was in charge of more than 20 000 Red Guards who supported the Bolsheviks. When he was elected as chairperson of the Petrograd soviet, he was able to make more detailed plans for taking over Petrograd. Four days before the Bolshevik take-over, most of the government troops in Petrograd switched their support to the Petrograd soviet. Two days later, the Bolshevik Red Guards took control of key buildings, bridges, railway stations etc. in the capital city.

People and power

Russia 1918-1923

g **C** To be able to answer questions on content relating to Russia 1918-1923, you should know about the following:

- the Bolshevik government
- Civil War between the Reds (or Bolsheviks, or Communists) and the Whites.
- activities of the Bolshevik (or Communist) government under Lenin, as shown by:
  - War Communism
  - New Economic Policy.

f To be able to answer questions on content relating to Russia 1918-1923, you should know about the following:

- the effects of civil war on Russian peasants
- Lenin and the Bolshevik government of 1917
- War Communism.

You should know the following background:

The Bolsheviks signed a truce with the Germans in December 1917 and a peace treaty in March 1918. The Bolsheviks had promised 'peace' and they were forced to agree to tough terms demanded by the Germans in the Treaty of Brest-Litovsk.
An end to the war with Germany would be popular with most Russians, and the Bolsheviks would be able to concentrate their efforts on consolidating and extending their power over Russian territory not handed over to the Germans. However, the terms of the Treaty of Brest-Litovsk were so harsh that even some Bolsheviks opposed signing the treaty, and by the summer of 1918 a civil war had broken out between the Bolsheviks and their opponents known as the 'Whites' who received aid from Russia's former allies (the UK, France, Japan and the USA).

The FactZone looks at the Civil War and War Communism.

The practice questions focus on Enquiry Skills at General and Credit levels.

Civil War 1918-1920

March 1918   The Treaty of Brest-Litovsk ended Russia's involvement in the First World War but resulted in Russia losing 74% of its iron and coal mines, 27% of its farm land, 26% of its railways and 26% of its population (due to change of nationality) to Germany. Also, the treaty angered the Social Revolutionaries who quit the coalition with the Bolsheviks (or Communists).

May 1918   The Czech Legion, made up of 45 000 prisoners of war, seized the Trans-Siberian railway and many towns along it. Enemies of the Bolsheviks used this opportunity to form White (or anti-Bolshevik) armies, and attack Moscow. This was the beginning of the Civil War.

December 1918 Troops from the UK, France, USA, Japan, Poland and Finland were sent to help the Whites. This foreign intervention turned many Russians against the Whites.

1919–1920   The Civil War was fought on several fronts. By early 1920, the Bolsheviks (or Communists), known as the Reds, controlled the central areas and were gaining the upper hand. The foreign troops began to withdraw. The Reds had won the Civil War.

War Communism

War Communism was the name given to the economic policies introduced by Lenin and the Communists (also known as Bolsheviks) during the Civil War. In order to win the Civil War, the Communists decided to take complete control of the economy in the areas of the country that they controlled, from farming to manufacturing to trading.

1) This meant that the Communists fixed the price of food. Farmers who refused to sell at those prices were imprisoned or killed. Because food remained in short supply, it was rationed by the Communists. Despite this, famine became a fact of life during the Civil War for many Russians.

2) Money was allowed to lose value, and barter (or the exchange of goods) was encouraged.

3) The Communists allowed some workers to take control of their factories through their councils (or local soviets), as their owners and managers had either fled abroad or had joined the Whites, the opponents of the Communists (or Reds). Large factories and key industries were controlled directly by the Communist government which made strikes illegal and forced people to work in factories to make up for labour shortages.

War Communism failed to solve the economic problems facing the areas controlled by the Communists. Fuel and food were in short supply in the towns and cities, and famine and disease quickly spread throughout the country areas. As people began to rebel against these unpopular policies, and the Red Guards and Cheka (or secret police) units found it increasingly difficult to keep the peasants and workers under control, the policy was abandoned and replaced by the New Economic Policy in 1921.

The New Economic Policy was a retreat from the more radical ideas represented by War Communism. Lenin had realised that Russia's many social and economic problems would not be solved quickly. However, in 1923, Lenin's health deteriorated and he died in January 1924. Trotsky, who had supported Lenin throughout this period, lost any influence he had over policy in 1925. He was expelled from the Communist Party in 1925, exiled in 1927 and assassinated by a Soviet agent in 1940.

People and power

Enquiry Skills

◉ Comparing sources

You could be asked to compare the evidence in more than one source, e.g. where they agree or disagree and the evidence or reasons for this, or the usefulness or value of two sources.

Here are two sources about the Civil War.

Source A is a cartoon of three White Generals, produced by the Bolsheviks in 1919. The dogs are named Denikin, Kolchak and Yudenich and they are controlled by foreign powers (France, the UK and the USA).

Source B is a map of the Civil War in Russia.

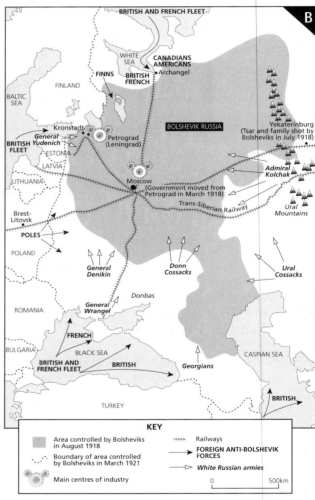

> **! REMEMBER**
> If the question refers to two sources, make clear references to both sources.

> ◉ **C** *To what extent do Sources A and B agree about the White forces in the Civil War in Russia? (4)*

> **! REMEMBER**
> At Credit level, give a balanced answer by pointing out similarities and differences between the information in the sources.

Similarities: both sources give the names of the White generals. Both sources refer to the foreign countries involved: the cartoon shows characters representing Britain, France and the USA controlling the dogs; the map refers to the foreign anti-Bolshevik forces including the British and French.

Differences: Source A is an example of Bolshevik propaganda as it suggests that the White generals were controlled by foreign powers (this is probably a biased point of view). Source B shows that the foreign powers sent troops and ships to Russia, while Source A shows them keeping their distance.

Here are two sources about the New Economic Policy.

Source C is a table of production figures that tells us about the effects of the New Economic Policy.

Table of production figures, Russia, 1913–1926						
	1913	1921	1922	1923	1925	1926
Grain (million tonnes)	80	37	50	57	73	77
Cattle (millions)	59		46		62	
Pigs (millions)	20		12		22	
Coal (million tonnes)	29	9	10	14	18	27
Steel (million tonnes)	4	0.2	0.7	0.7	2	3

Source D is an extract from the memoirs of a Bolshevik published in 1992, telling us about the introduction of the New Economic Policy.

There wasn't a scrap of food in the country. We were down to our last small piece of bread per person, then suddenly they announced the NEP. Cafés started opening, restaurants, factories went back into private hands; it was capitalism. The papers kept quoting Lenin – 'Two steps forward, one step back'; that's all very well but in my eyes what was happening was what I'd struggled against. I can remember the years 1921 and 1922; we used to discuss NEP for hours on end at party meetings. Most people supported Lenin, others said he was wrong; many tore up their party cards.

People and power

◎ *Highlight any points in the sources or in the background information provided, using one colour for similarities and another for differences.*

⑦ *Think about the nature of the sources. How useful and/or reliable are they?*

Source C contains facts and figures, while Source D contains a man's opinion. Remember that the man who wrote Source D was a Bolshevik, so his information may be biased and unreliable, although it is a useful eyewitness account of living through the crises of 1922.

Practice questions

C **1** To what extent do Sources C and D agree that the New Economic Policy was a success? (4)

g **2** How useful is Source D as evidence of the success of the New Economic Policy? (4)

Write one or two paragraphs to answer either question. Allow yourself 10 minutes.

Russia 1924-1941

g **c** To be able to answer questions on content relating to Russia 1924-1941, you should know about the following:

- the activities of the Communist government under Stalin, as demonstrated by:
  - Five Year Plans
  - collectivisation
  - political purges.

f To be able to answer questions on content relating to Russia 1924-1941, you should know about the following:

- Stalin and the Five Year Plans
- collectivisation
- Stalin and the kulaks.

You should know the following background:

Stalin led the Soviet Union by eliminating all opposition to his rule, real or imagined. He was able to force his ideas on the Communist Party from his position as Party Secretary. From 1928, Stalin set out to achieve his aim of 'Socialism in One Country' (i.e. the Soviet Union) through his collectivisation of agriculture and the Five Year Plans for industry.

In 1929, Trotsky was exiled from the Soviet Union. In 1933, 1936 and 1938, Stalin organised a series of trials in which his opponents were accused of treason and condemned to death or forced labour in camps. 'Yezhovshchina' is a Russian term for the 'Great Purge' in the Soviet Union, taken from the name of the head of Stalin's secret police (the NKVD), N. I. Yezhov. He supervised the elimination of any opposition within the Communist Party and the Red Army, real or imagined, e.g. the Chief of the General Staff and 400 out of 700 generals were eliminated. There are no precise figures for the number of Soviet citizens who suffered, and often died, to maintain Stalin's hold on power, but it is probably tens of thousands.

In 1941, Stalin became Prime Minister (Chairman of the Council of Ministers) and he remained in this post where he ruled directly, rather than indirectly through the Communist Party organisation, until his death in 1953.

The FactZone looks at collectivisation, industrialisation and the Five Year Plans. The practice questions focus on Enquiry Skills at General level.

Collectivisation

1924–1928 Stalin continued Lenin's NEP (New Economic Policy); the peasants retained private ownership of their land and were allowed to sell food for profit. The speed of industrial development was slow. Stalin opposed calls for change.

1928–1941 Stalin was worried about Russia's economic backwardness in agriculture and industry. He feared attack by capitalist countries (particularly Germany after 1933), so he decided to modernise rapidly.

Industrial development needed more factory workers and fewer, but more efficient, peasant farmers. However, agriculture was producing two million tonnes less grain than was needed in 1928. Stalin decided that 25 million individual peasant farms should be joined together into 250 000 state collective farms (kolkhozes). Peasants were to share equipment, animals and land in each kolkhoz. Machine Tractor Stations were set up to provide tractors and repair machinery. This process of modernising Russian agriculture was called collectivisation.

Results

■ In 1930, many better-off peasants (kulaks) slaughtered their animals rather than hand them over to the collective farms. Stalin decided to destroy the kulaks as a class: 1.5 million out of 5 million kulaks were forced to move to poorer parts of the Soviet Union. Many who resisted being moved were executed.
■ By 1935, 85% of all land had been collectivised.
■ The destruction and chaos caused by collectivisation led to a drop in food production, and famine in parts of the Soviet Union during 1932-1933. Food production levels did not return to 1928 figures until 1939.

Industrialisation and the Five Year Plans

1928–1932 First Five Year Plan: this plan was drawn up by Gosplan which was the state planning commission. The plan concentrated on heavy industry (iron, steel, coal, electricity, oil, machinery). These industries were given high targets for increased production.

1933–1937 Second Five Year Plan: this plan continued the emphasis on heavy industry, especially tractors for collective farms. To encourage workers to work harder, bonus or extra payments were made to those workers who exceeded the targets set for them. Groups of specially selected workers became heroes, and they were used as examples to motivate other workers. One of the best known of these workers was Stakhanov, a miner who produced a record amount of coal in one day in 1935.

1938–1941 Third Five Year Plan: this plan concentrated on light industry (consumer goods). This was quite successful, but was abandoned in 1940 due to fear of invasion. Production was switched to armaments and munitions to prepare the Soviet Union for war.

Results

■ Despite problems, industrial production increased greatly (though most targets were set too high to be met) and the Soviet Union became a major industrial state.
■ Many new canals, railways, dams and industrial centres were built.

People and power

Enquiry Skills

◉ Evaluating sources

74

REMEMBER
Note that biased or unreliable sources can be useful as evidence of propaganda used at a certain time.

Here are two sources about the collectivisation.

Source A is a photograph of a Soviet peasant taken in 1923.

Source B is an extract from Stalin's explanation of the new policy of collectivisation, written in 1929.

> *A radical change is taking place in the development of our agriculture from small, backward, individual farming. We are advancing full steam ahead along the path of industrialisation to Socialism, leaving behind the age-long 'Russian' backwardness. We are becoming a country of metal, a country of cars, a country of tractors, and when we have put the USSR in a car, and a peasant on a tractor, let the capitalists try to overtake us.*

◉ ⑨ *How useful is Source A as evidence to explain why the collectivisation of agriculture was introduced by Stalin in 1929? (4)*

Source A was produced in 1923 rather than 1929, so conditions might have improved by then. It is useful in that it shows how backward agriculture could be in the 1920s. The source is propaganda and the scene may have been staged for the camera.

REMEMBER
Mention the date if it is given, or give some idea of when you think the source was produced, but don't write 'at the time'.

◉ ⑨ *How useful is Source B as evidence to explain why the collectivisation of agriculture was introduced by Stalin in 1929? (4)*

Source B was produced just after the introduction of collectivisation. Stalin provides us with the reasons why he introduced collectivisation. He may be trying to justify the policy, and/or hide any negative aspects of the policy's effects (the source is probably biased).

Here are two sources about industrialisation and the Five Year Plans.

Source C is a Soviet cartoon from 1933 showing a foreign capitalist's anger at the achievements of the first Five Year Plan.

REMEMBER
Think about what each source tells us, and whether or not this information is useful. Note when the source was written, who produced it and why.

75

Source D is a table of industrial output, 1927-1940, compiled from Soviet and Western sources by an economic historian.

	1927	1930	1932	1935	1937	1940
Coal (million tonnes)	36	61	65	102	130	152
Steel (million tonnes)	3	5	6	13	18	18
Oil (million tonnes)	12	17	21	24	26	26
Electricity (million kWh)	18	22	20	45	80	90

Practice questions

g 1 How useful is Source C as evidence of the success of the first Five Year Plan? (4)

g 2 How useful is Source D as evidence of the success of the plans up to 1940? (4)

Write one or two paragraphs to answer either question. Allow yourself 10 minutes.

People and power

The Weimar Republic 1919-1933

g **C** To be able to answer questions on the Weimar Republic 1919-1933, you should know about the following:

• the effects of the First World War on Germany (huge number of casualties; food and other shortages; the spread of disease and Spanish influenza; growing discontent, e.g. naval mutinies at Kiel)

• the setting up of the Weimar Republic and the drafting of its constitution

• the Treaty of Versailles ('Diktat', i.e. dictated peace; War Guilt; the 'November Criminals')

• opposition to the Weimar Republic as seen in the Kapp Putsch and the Beer Hall Putsch

• economic problems of the Weimar Republic 1919-1933 (hyper-inflation in 1923, following the French invasion of the Ruhr; the Stresemann years and reliance on American loans; the Great Depression, mass unemployment and the rise in support for the Communists and the Nazis)

• the collapse of the Weimar Republic (coalition governments; rule by presidential decree; the 1932 elections).

f To be able to answer questions on Weimar Germany 1919-1933, you should know about the following:

• the fall of the Kaiser in 1918

• the Treaty of Versailles and German opposition to its terms

• the rights of individual citizens in the Weimar Republic

• the Beer Hall Putsch, 1923

• the effects of inflation on standards of living in 1923.

The name 'Weimar Republic' is used by historians to describe the German Federal Republic from November 1918 until January 1933, when Hitler became Chancellor. Following the revolution in Germany at the end of the First World War that resulted from the abdication of Kaiser Wilhelm II, the new republic's National Assembly (elected by everyone over the age of twenty) met at the town of Weimar to draw up the republic's new constitution. It was hoped that by holding their meetings in Weimar, the politicians would reduce the influence of Berlin's political extremists on the new constitution.

The FactZone deals with the setting up of the Weimar Republic and its constitution, focusing on the Weimar Constitution and potential problems facing the Weimar Republic.

You need to learn these key facts:

The Weimar Constitution

February 1919   Ebert, a Social Democrat, was elected President of the new republican government of Germany.

August 1919   The constitution of the new republic was drawn up in the town of Weimar and accepted by Germany's leading political parties.

The new constitution set out the rules that made Germany a democracy. Before 1919, the Kaiser (or Emperor) and his advisers controlled the government, foreign affairs and the armed forces.
■ The head of state in the Weimar Republic was the President, not a Kaiser (or Emperor).
■ The President was elected by everybody over twenty, in a secret ballot, and remained in office for seven years.
■ The Weimar Constitution set up a new Reichstag (or parliament) elected by everybody over twenty, in a secret ballot, at least every four years.
■ Seats in the Reichstag were awarded by proportional representation (PR). That meant that a political party that won 35% of the votes in a general election, for example, would be awarded 35% of the seats in the Reichstag. This made it nearly impossible for one party to gain an overall majority in the Reichstag, and governments tended to be coalition governments made up of several parties.
■ The Chancellor (or Prime Minister) was supposed to represent the largest group of deputies or members of parliament in the Reichstag.
■ The Weimar Constitution promised every German 'Fundamental Rights': individual rights of a citizen such as no-one could be arrested without a trial; police could not enter someone's house without a warrant; workers could join trade unions; there would be no government censorship of newspapers and magazines.
■ The Weimar Republic was a federal system in which power was shared between the central government based in Berlin, and the 18 new Länder (or state) governments.

Potential problems facing the Weimar Republic

■ Although the Kaiser had resigned (or abdicated), the important people who had supported him remained in key positions. Government officials, judges, chiefs of police and army officers who had no respect for democracy kept their jobs.
■ Germany's democratic politicians were forced to sign the 'Diktat' or Treaty of Versailles by Germany's enemies. As a result, supporters of the ex-Kaiser and opponents of the new government called democratic politicians the 'November Criminals' because they has accepted defeat at the hands of the Allies.
■ In the four difficult years from 1919-1923, PR meant that Germany had nine short-lived coalition governments. Many Germans began to associate democracy with political instability and weakness, as well as defeat and humiliation.
■ Article 48 of the constitution gave the German President the power to announce a 'state of emergency' and make laws by himself, in place of the Reichstag.

People and power

Enquiry Skills

The Weimar Constitution

This source is a table showing the results of the elections in Germany, 1919-1928.

	% of votes won				
	1919	**1920**	**1924**		**1928**
			May	*Dec*	
German Communist Party (KPD)		2	12	9	11
Social Democratic Party (SPD)	38	21	21	26	30
German Democratic Party (DDP)	19	8	6	6	5
Centre Party	20	18	17	8	15
German People's Party (DVP)	4	14	9	10	9
German Nationalist Party (DNVP)	10	15	19	21	14
Nazi Party (NSDAP)			7	3	2
Other (minor) parties	9	22	9	7	14

! REMEMBER Always use any information that the examiner provides about a source.

◎ **9** *How useful is this source for studying German politics in the 1920s? (3)*

You can begin your answer to the question by writing something like 'This source is quite useful because ...'

Relate your answer to the second half of the question by discussing the light the source throws on German politics in the 1920s. Identify points such as: the SPD, Centre Party and the DNVP dominated elections at this time; the Nazi Party was an insignificant political force up to 1928.

You can bring in recalled information such as:

■ proportional representation made it difficult for a single party to gain an overall majority

■ close results led to frequent coalition governments.

Mention the fact that the results in the table can only tell us part of the story since political history is about personalities, crises, decisions taken, agreements made etc.

Evaluating sources

When asked about how useful a source is:

■ say whether or not the source is useful, i.e. does it help us to better understand what happened or what people thought?

■ provide evidence for that answer by referring to features in any source, such as authorship (who produced it?), purpose (why was it produced?), date (when was it produced?) and detail (what information does it contain and how accurate do you think it is?)

■ when the source is a map or a table of information, concentrate on the detail

■ at Credit level, try to mention the source or sources' strengths and weaknesses, e.g. gaps in the evidence, signs of bias and/or inaccuracy or even exaggeration.

When asked about how reliable a source is:

■ say whether or not you think the source is reliable, i.e. a trustworthy source of accurate information or opinion (in Unit I, you will be asked about two sources)

■ provide evidence for that answer, by referring to features in any source such as authorship (who produced it?), purpose (why was it produced?), date (when was it produced?) and detail (what information does it contain and how accurate do you think it is?)

■ at Credit level, try to mention the source or sources' strengths and weaknesses, e.g. gaps in the evidence, signs of bias and/or inaccuracy, or even exaggeration.

As a rule, sources produced by Hitler and the Nazi Party will be biased, and often full of lies and offensive comments about their political enemies. These sources may not be reliable but that does not mean that theses sources are not useful or valuable to the historian. Evaluate these sources in the same way that you evaluate any other source.

■ Ask yourself 'Is this source useful and valuable?' and 'Is this source reliable?'

■ Provide evidence for your answer by referring to features in the source.

Who produce the source and what is their point of view? For example, is the author biased?

Why was the source produced and who was meant to look at it or read it?

When was the source produced and why is this important? For example, it many have been produced at an important turning point in the history of the Nazis.

What information does the source contain? For example, does it contain fact or opinion? Sometimes, the facts may be accurate but the opinion of the author is biased. Often, the facts and the opinion will provide evidence of bias and exaggeration.

The rise of the Nazis

g **C** To be able to answer questions on the rise of the Nazis, you should know about the following:

● the Munich Beer Hall Putsch, 1923 (including Hitler's trial and imprisonment)

● Nazi beliefs ('Mein Kampf' or 'My Struggle')

● the impact of the Great Depression after 1929 (mass unemployment; increasing support for political extremists at elections)

● the Nazis' rise to power (collapse of Weimar democracy; the President's use of Article 48; elections 1930-1932; political deals; the Reichstag Fire)

● the formation and characteristics of the Nazi government.

f To be able to answer questions on the rise of the Nazis, you should know about the following:

● the Munich Beer Hall Putsch, 1923

● the Reichstag Fire, 1933.

You should know the following background:

Hitler was not alone in his hatred of Jews. In the 1920s and 30s, there were many people in Europe who disliked Jewish people (i.e. they were anti-Semitic). In fact, Jews had been persecuted in many parts of Europe for centuries. Like many other people at that time, Hitler claimed that the German people were 'Aryans'. The Aryans were the 'Master Race' and all other races of people were inferior. As far as Hitler was concerned, Jews belonged to an inferior but dangerous race that threatened the Aryans. Hitler claimed that Jews were the chief cause of Germany's defeat in the First World War, and were responsible for Germany's problems after 1918. When Hitler became Chancellor and President of Germany, he and his supporters in the Nazi Party were able to use their power to persecute Jews in the years leading up the outbreak of the Second World War.

The FactZone deals with Hitler's rise to power 1929-1934.

The activities look at Knowledge and Understanding at General level.

🔍 You need to learn these key facts:

Hitler's rise to power 1929-1934

1929   Financial problems in the USA (the Wall Street Crash) led to a worldwide economic crisis (the Great Depression) affecting international trade. Unemployment in Germany rose to more than 5 million by 1932.

1930   As the economic crisis deepened, it created political instability:
■ President Hindenburg used Article 48 of the constitution to make laws on behalf of Chancellors unable to win the support of an overall majority in the Reichstag
■ support for parties that did not support democratic government began to increase
■ as support for the Communists increased in Germany, the Nazis received financial support from businessmen.

1932   This was a crucial year in Hitler's rise to power.
■ Hitler stood as a candidate in the presidential election, receiving 13 million votes. He lost to Hindenburg who received 19 million votes, but he was seen now as a major political figure in Germany.
■ In July, the Nazis became the largest single party in the Reichstag with 230 seats (in November, the Nazis won 34 fewer seats, while the Communists increased their share of seats in the Reichstag to 100).
■ Von Papen became angry and bitter when Von Schleicher took over from him as Chancellor (i.e. Prime Minister). Von Papen was able to persuade President Hindenburg to consider the possibility of a Hitler-Von Papen government, supported by the Nazis as the largest party in the Reichstag.

1933   In January, President Hindenburg appointed Hitler as Chancellor. When Hitler was appointed Chancellor, he used his power to strengthen his own position, and to weaken that of his opponents.
■ The Nazis were assisted by the Reichstag Fire, shortly before the election called by Hitler for March 1933.
■ Only the Nazis and their nationalist allies were able to campaign freely for the election.
■ As Communists who were elected could not take their seats in the Reichstag, the Nazis had an overall majority.
■ The Enabling Bill passed by the Reichstag in March 1933 gave Hitler the power to make laws without the Reichstag. As this Bill changed the constitution, the Nazis needed the votes of the Centre Party who decided to support the Bill.

1934   In June, Hitler ordered the execution of any potential rivals from within his own ranks. Roehm and other SA leaders were murdered in cold blood. Gregor Strasser and Von Schleicher were executed, too. At the same time, von Papen was forced to resign. In August, Hitler took the final step to total power when President Hindenburg died. Hitler was proclaimed Führer of the Germain Reich, as Head of State (President and Chancellor) and Supreme Commander of Germany's armed forces. German troops had to take a personal oath of loyalty to Hitler. In the space of eighteen months, Hitler had taken advantage of the invitation to lead a coalition government, and had become the most powerful man in a one-party state.

Knowledge and Understanding

◉ The Nazi Party in the 1920s

This source is an extract from a letter written by Hitler in 1923 when he was imprisoned in Landsberg Castle.

> *When I resume active work it will be necessary to pursue a new policy. Instead of working to achieve power by an armed coup, we will have to hold our noses and enter the Reichstag against the Catholic and Marxist members. If outvoting them takes longer than outshooting them, at least the result will be guaranteed by their own constitution. Any lawful process is slow. Sooner or later we will have a majority, and after that – Germany!*

(?) *Take a highlighter pen and underline these words and phrases from the source: 'necessary to pursue a new policy', 'we will have to hold our noses and enter the Reichstag', 'outvoting them', 'the result will be guaranteed by their own constitution', 'we will have a majority', 'after that – Germany!' Consider their significance.*

◉ **g** *Why did Hitler change the Nazi Party's organisation and political programme after 1923? (3)*

To answer this General level question, you need to identify at least two main points in the source such as:

■ Hitler abandoned the idea of seizing power by military force

■ Hitler decided to win power through building up the Nazi Party's representation in the Reichstag

■ Hitler had decided to gain power in a legal manner by winning a majority in the Reichstag.

You also need to mention one piece of relevant recalled information such as:

- Hitler needed time to rebuild the Nazi Party after the disastrous Beer Hall Putsch (his attempt in 1923 to overthrow the state government of Bavaria as the first step towards marching on Berlin)

- the Nazi Party was split after the Beer Hall Putsch and needed to be rebuilt as a political force

- Hitler recognised the need to attract support from wealthy people

- when Hitler was in prison, the Dawes Plan helped the German government to overcome its economic problems

- economic stability between 1924 and 1928 would make it very difficult for an extremist party to gain sufficient support to be able to seize power by a military coup.

◎ *Highlight the information in the tips above in two colours showing general factors and factors relating to the Nazi Party itself.*

Ⓒ One Knowledge and Understanding question in the Credit paper will be worth eight marks. For this question, remember the following points.

- Your short essay should be two, three or four paragraphs in length. It should take you about ten to fifteen minutes to write under exam conditions.

- You should end your short essay with a brief, but balanced conclusion: it is a good idea to begin your final paragraph with the words 'In conclusion ...'

- Try to practise writing short essay answers on topics from Units I, II and III as part of your revision. An eight-mark Knowledge and Understanding practice question is given below.

⁇ *Write a list of key points to use in answer to the practice question below. These might include:*
  - worldwide economic crisis led to high unemployment in Germany
  - President used Article 48 to make laws by decree
  - growth in support for extremist parties, including the Nazis
  - many Germans feared the growing support for the Communists
  - the Nazis had enough financial support to pay for propaganda and publicity
  - Hitler stood as a presidential candidate in 1932, becoming a major political figure.

! **REMEMBER**
When revising, read over any difficult topics you are worried about and make a note of questions to ask your teacher as soon as possible.

83

People and power

Practice question

Ⓒ Explain why support for the Nazis grew rapidly after 1929. (8)

Write a short essay of several paragraphs to answer this revision question. Allow yourself ten to fifteen minutes.

Nazi Germany 1933-1939

g **c** To be able to answer questions on Germany 1933-1939, you should know about the following:
• the Nazis' destruction of Weimar democracy (Reichstag Fire; taking over of the Länder, or German states; the Enabling Act; the banning of other parties)
• the Night of the Long Knives; Hitler becomes Führer (or leader) of Germany
• the establishment of the Nazi police state
• economic policies (National Labour Service, public works, rearmament and conscription)
• Nazi persecution of Jews, 1933-1939
• youth movements and education in Nazi Germany
• Nazi propaganda and militarism
• opposition to National Socialism from socialists, communists and the churches.

f To be able to answer questions on on Germany 1933-1939, you should know about the following:
• the main features of Nazi government, 1933-1939
• how the Nazis treated the Jews
• Nazi youth movements
• the Nuremberg rallies.

You should know how Hitler was able to reduce Germany's unemployment figures so quickly.

• The Nazis came to power at a time when the world economy was recovering. The German economy benefited from an increase in world trade, leading to more jobs in manufacturing.
• A house-building programme led to more jobs in construction.
• The government launched a road-building programme that created thousands of jobs.
• Many Jews were sacked or forced to become unemployed, and they were not counted when the unemployment figures were announced.
• Women were excluded from the unemployment figures, while many unemployed men found work by taking jobs that had been done by women.
• Part-time workers were counted as being in full-time employment.
• Compulsory military service (conscription) meant that thousands of young men were no longer unemployed or in full-time employment.

The FactZones deal with potential opponents of Nazi rule, Nazi persecution of Jews 1933-1939 and youth movements in Nazi Germany.
The activities and practice exam question focus on Knowledge and Understanding at Credit level.

You need to learn these key facts:

Potential opponents of Nazi rule

■ As soon as the Nazis came to power, their first targets were the Communists and Social Democrats. These political parties were seen as major threats to Nazi power and they were outlawed as soon as possible. Soon after, only the Nazi party was allowed to function as a political party.

■ Trade unions were seen as a threat to Nazi power. The larger trade unions were closely linked to the Social Democrats and the Nazis feared their potential power. They decided to smash the trade unions as soon as possible.

■ The civil service and legal profession were regarded as possible sources of opposition to Nazi power and great efforts were made to ensure that civil servants and those in the legal profession were loyal to the Nazi regime.

■ The armed forces were seen by the Nazis as a possible source of opposition to Nazi plans and programmes. The Army High Command escaped the policy of 'co-ordination' that applied to other organisations and institutions that were possible sources of opposition to the Nazi regime, but Hitler insisted on an oath of loyalty being sworn by the armed forces in 1934.

■ Christian churches in Germany were seen as possible sources of criticism and opposition to many Nazi policies, so the Nazis worked hard to weaken the influence of the Catholic and various Protestant churches over public opinion.

Nazi persecution of Jews 1933-1939

1933   The SA were ordered to organise a national boycott of Jewish shops and businesses. Jews were sacked from important jobs (Civil Service, the law, universities and schools, newspapers, radio and film).

1934   All Jewish shops were marked with a yellow star or the word 'Juden' (Jews). Jews had to sit on separate seats on buses, trams, trains and in parks. In schools, Jewish children began to be victimised.

1935   The Nuremberg Laws came into effect: German Jews were no longer allowed to marry 'Aryans' (German non-Jews). Jews were encouraged to leave Germany as long as they could find a sympathetic country that would allow them to enter as refugees.

1938   After a Nazi official was shot by a Jew, the SA destroyed shops and synagogues and killed about 1000 Jews. Around 30 000 Jews were arrested. This event is known as 'Krystallnacht' ('Crystal Night' or the 'Night of Broken Glass').

Remember that Hitler gained control over most of Europe's Jewish population by 1941. The 'Final Solution' to what the Nazis considered to be their Jewish 'problem' led to the deaths of at least six million Jews by 1945. Together with other victims of Nazi hatred such as gypsies and homosexuals, millions of Jews were starved, denied medical treatment, beaten, tortured, shot and gassed by the Nazis and their allies throughout Europe. This phase of Nazi terror has become known as the Holocaust.

Knowledge and Understanding

◉ Nazi persecution of Jews 1933–1939

A photograph of Nazis enforcing a boycott of Jewish shops in 1933.

! REMEMBER Check your notes and text book for additional information.

◎ **C** *Describe how Jews were treated in Nazi Germany in the years 1933-1939. (8)*

It should take you ten to fifteen minutes to write your essay. Try to write three or four paragraphs on the main developments. This particular question does not require a conclusion.

Try to remember the main developments without looking at the FactZone, then check back to see if you have missed anything.

To answer this question you need to focus on the main Nazi laws and actions up to 1939 (don't mention the Final Solution and the Holocaust as they are outside the period of the question).

Nazi policies for young people

Once Hitler became Führer, all youth organisations were taken over by the Nazis.

■ Young people were encouraged to join the 'Hitler-Jugend' (Hitler Youth Movement) originally set up in 1925. In 1936, the movement had approximately four million members, as other youth movements had been closed down. In fact, membership of the Hitler Youth was almost compulsory for young Germans, aged 10 to 18.

■ The movement was divided into five different sections, with separate groups for boys and girls.

– boys could belong to the Little Fellows from 6-10, the Youth Folk from 10-14, and the Hitler Youth from 14-18.

– for girls, there were the Young Girls from 10-14, and the German Girls from 14-18.

■ Boys were prepared for military service, and children of both sexes were encouraged to report on any adults, including neighbours, teachers and family members, who made critical comments about the Nazi government.

■ Members attended youth camps every year and there were special schools for members who received top marks in exams called Adolf Hitler Schools and Order Castles.

Hitler Youth greeting their Führer, 1935.

People and power

Knowledge and Understanding

⊡ ◉ Nazi policies for young people

A photograph of a Hitler Youth Camp at Nuremberg in 1934.

❗ REMEMBER
The question asks about boys and girls, so make sure you write about both sexes.

◎ *Plan three or four paragraphs for the practice question below.*

◎ *Work out how to write a balanced answer by showing that some young people resisted Nazi policies and propaganda. Don't just write about the Nazis' plans.*

❓ *Think about how you will write a conclusion to this question.*

Practice question

C Explain why the lives of boys and girls changed in Nazi Germany, 1933–1939. (8)

Write a short essay of several paragraphs to answer this question. Allow yourself ten to fifteen minutes.

Sample answers

These answers are not 'perfect' answers, but are designed to demonstrate how the answer tips can be used to write answers that should gain the marks that your hard work and effort deserve. In most cases, you should be able to come up with alternative pieces of evidence to back up the answers provided.

UNIT I: CONTEXT A
p15
Why did the radicals want Parliament to be reformed? (4)
The radicals wanted Parliament to be reformed because hardly anyone could vote for a Member of Parliament (4000 voters out of two million people). Apart from Edinburgh, Scotland's cities and burghs were combined into groups of four or five to share MPs. A large city like Glasgow was treated the same as a tiny burgh with a population of a few hundred people. In the burghs, only council members could vote for MPs. In the counties, six counties took it in turns to elect three MPs at every other General Election.

p16
How useful is Source A for investigating changes in farming methods in Scotland during the period 1750-1800? (3)
This source is quite useful. It describes only one county, but describes the changes that have taken place by the end of the period 1750-1800, such as the enclosing of fields, the introduction of new crop rotations and the improved selection of seeds. These improvements were introduced in other counties at the same time. The author possibly is biased when he claims that this Scottish county is the envy of the richest counties in England, never mind in Scotland.

p17
What evidence in Source A agrees with the view that farming methods in Scotland changed in the period 1750-1800?
What evidence in Source B disagrees with the view that farming methods in Scotland changed in the period 1750-1800? (5)
Source A says that wheat, oats, barley, turnips and potatoes are being grown. Fields have been enclosed and subdivided.

Crops are rotated so that the fertility of the soil is not exhausted. The soil is tilled, spread with manure, weeded and watered. Source B says that cattle and sheep die in winter due to a shortage of grass and hay. Much of the land is wasteground covered in stones and couch grass. Pasture and meadow lands are strewed with the carcasses of dead sheep.

Practice question, p17
How far do you agree that farming methods in Scotland changed in the period 1750-1800? You must use evidence from the sources and your own knowledge to come to a conclusion. (4)
I agree that farming methods changed, to a large extent, in many parts of Scotland. New crops and crop rotations were introduced as farmers planted new varieties of wheat, oats, barley, turnips and potatoes. Land was enclosed and larger fields were created. Farmers tilled, spread with manure, weeded and watered the soil in these enclosed fields. These changes meant that many small farms were swallowed up by larger farms, and many farmers moved to the towns and cities to look for work, or emigrated. In some places, the soil was too poor to make it worthwhile to introduce improvements. Old farming methods continued to be used, and a shortage of feed for cattle and sheep remained a problem in winter and spring in some areas.

UNIT I: CONTEXT B
Practice questions, p21
1 How useful are Sources A and B for investigating whether industrial growth was responsible for the rise in population of Scotland's towns and cities? (4)
Source A is useful because it describes the author's own family's move to Glasgow from a farm in the Lothians. This person was writing in 1838 and was describing how cottagers were moving to large towns at this time as a result of farming improvements. These farmers were being driven out by the need to improve farming methods to feed Scotland's growing population. Industrial growth meant that the author's father could become a mechanic in Glasgow. However, this source suggests that farmers were

being pushed out by economic and technological change, rather than being pulled by the new employment opportunities provided by industrial growth.
Source B is useful because it describes, in detail, the rise in population of Scotland's great towns. It provides information about the rate of population increase in Scotland's larger towns and cities, and compares their relative growth. It is clear that Glasgow's growth rate was greater than that of any other large town or city. As a major centre of industry, Glasgow's population growth must be linked to its industrial development. Not every Scottish town was an industrial centre, and the source notes that only one-third of Scots lived in towns with populations greater than 5000 people.

2 What evidence in the sources supports the view that industrial growth was responsible for the rise in population of Scotland's towns and cities?
What evidence in the sources suggests that industrial growth was not the only reason for the population rise in towns and cities? (6)
Evidence for the view that industrial growth was responsible for the rise in population of Scotland's towns and cities: author's father moved from his farm to become a mechanic in Glasgow some time before 1838 (Source A); many cottagers moved to large towns in the years before 1838 suggesting that they were looking for work in the new industries after they had been driven out of farming by changing methods (Source A); Glasgow grew in size by more than one-third between 1831 and 1841 probably due to industrial growth (Source B); the coal, iron and textile industries of Glasgow and Lanarkshire attracted tens of thousands of Irish immigrants (Source C); the cotton industry of the west of Scotland attracted Irish immigrants to Glasgow (Source C).
Evidence for the view that industrial growth was not the only reason for the population rise in towns and cities: author's father pushed out of farming by improvements, so moved to town looking for any work that was available (Source A); many cottagers who were being driven out of farming by improvements were looking for work at that time, so moved

to towns (Source A); only 35% of the population lived in towns with over 5000 inhabitants suggesting that most people continued to live in small towns, where farming or small-scale industry were the main sources of employment (Source B); the decline of the linen and woollen industries in the north of Ireland encouraged many Irish people to move from Ireland to look for work (Source C).

3 To what extent did the growth of industry lead to the increase in the population of Scotland's towns and cities between 1830 and 1900? You must use evidence from the sources and your own knowledge to reach a balanced conclusion. (5)

Many farmers moved to large towns in the years before 1838 suggesting that they were looking for work in the new industries after they had been driven out of farming by changing methods. Glasgow grew in size by more than one-third between 1831 and 1841 probably due to industrial growth. At this time, the coal, iron and textile industries of Glasgow and Lanarkshire attracted tens of thousands of Irish immigrants to Scotland.

On the other hand, many people moved to towns and cities looking for work as they had been pushed out of farming by changes in methods. Farming methods were being improved to produce enough food to feed Scotland's fast-growing population at that time. Irish people moved to the British mainland looking for work as their linen and woollen industries declined. Then, in the 1840s and 1850s, thousands of Irish people moved to the British mainland to escape poverty and famine. These people tended to move to larger towns looking for work. However, most of the population continued to live in the country or in towns with under 5000 inhabitants.

In conclusion, the growth of industry was to a large extent responsible for the increase in the population of Scotland's towns and cities between 1830 and 1900. Other factors included farming improvements and Irish immigration.

UNIT I: CONTEXT C

p24

How useful is Source A for investigating the working conditions of women at home between 1930 and 1939? (3)
This source is quite useful. This woman is describing her life in a Scottish city in the 1930s. She lives in a city like so many Scots at that time. She is describing housework at a time when most men

didn't help around the house. Her new washing machine must have saved her a great deal of time and effort. Her new electric fire would have meant one less coal fire to worry about, and less coal and ash to carry in and out of the house. On the other hand, her memories would not be typical of most Scots at that time. Many families would not have been able to afford the new consumer goods that this woman bought to make life easier at home.

p25

What evidence is there in Source A to support the view that women's working conditions at home improved between 1930 and 1939?
What evidence is there in Source B to show that women still had to work hard around the home in the 1930s? (5)
Evidence in Source A to support the view that women's working conditions improved, 1930-1939:

Author's mother bought washing machine that would have made washing family's clothes less of a chore; she bought an electric fire that heated a bedroom, and meant that there was one less coal fire to light.

Evidence in Source B showing that women still had to work hard around the house, 1930-1939:

Most housewives had to work hard to clean and tidy small rooms; clothes, towels and sheets had to be washed by hand; work clothes had to be washed and dried nearly every day; water for cleaning had to be heated before every wash in the wash house boiler, or women had to take the laundry to a public wash house.

Practice question, p26

How far do you think that working conditions for women at home improved by the 1930s? Use evidence from the sources and your own knowledge to come to a conclusion. (4)
I think that working conditions for most women at home did not improve very much during the 1930s. Most housewives had to work hard to clean, tidy and heat small rooms. Clothes, towels and sheets had to be washed by hand, and work clothes had to be washed and dried nearly every day. Water for cleaning had to be heated before every wash in the wash house boiler, or women had to take the laundry to a public wash house. Some families could afford to buy some of the new labour-saving consumer goods such as washing machines, but most could not.

To make ends meet, more and more women were going out to work in factories and this meant that they had less time to complete their housework. At this time, men did not help much around the house and would not set foot inside a 'steamie'.

UNIT II: CONTEXT A

p30

How fully does the evidence in Source A explain the role of the great powers in preventing further war in Europe? You should use your own knowledge and give reasons for your answer. (4)
Source A, to some extent, explains the role of the great powers in preventing further war in Europe. It was written by Metternich in 1815, at the time when the great powers of Austria, Britain, Prussia and Russia had signed the Quadruple Alliance. Metternich played a key part in outlining what the role of the great powers should be in preventing war. He believed that the great powers had a responsibility to safeguard Europe's future stability and that none of the major powers should take any action that might lead to conflict without consulting the other powers first. However, the role of the great powers in preventing further war depended on the political priorities of each of them, and the extent to which these priorities might lead to conflict with their neighbours or the other major powers. These priorities are not set out in this source.

p31

To what extent do Sources A and B agree about the aims of the Congress System? (4)
To some extent, sources A and B agree about the aims of the Congress System. Both sources were written by Metternich so they should provide us with a good idea of his thoughts on the Congress System. Source B was written seven years after Source A and much had happened in those years to influence Metternich's thinking on this matter. In Source A, Metternich is giving advice to the great powers, while in Source B he is justifying the action taken by the Congress Powers to the Spanish government. Source A represents the theory behind the Congress System, and Source B tells us about the Congress System in action. In Source A, Metternich's priority is avoiding the outbreak of war, while in Source B his priority is preventing the spread of revolutionary ideas.

UNIT II: CONTEXT B

Practice question, p35
How fully do Sources A and B describe the layout of trench systems on the Western Front? You should use your own knowledge and give reasons for your answer. (4)
Sources A and B quite fully describe the layout of trench systems on the Western Front. Source A is a plan of a British or French trench system showing the location of no man's land, barbed wire defences, the front-line trench, communication trenches, support trench, reserve trench, artillery, battalion headquarters and railway communications. It illustrates the zig-zag layout of trench defences and the scale gives some idea of the distances involved. With a few modifications, the plan could be used to illustrate German defences, too. Source B is a photograph taken inside a trench on the Western Front, and it illustrates the main features of a typical British or French trench. The photograph appears to have been taken inside a trench during the war, and it shows a soldier on guard, while some other soldiers try to get some sleep. Again, this photograph could illustrate the interior of some German trenches as both sides often captured enemy trenches, and adapted them for their own use. However, background knowledge is needed to pick the details in the photograph out, such as the fire step the guard is standing on and the duck-board the man is lying on.

p37
How useful is this poster for studying the British government's methods of encouraging men to volunteer for the armed forces? (5)
This source is quite useful for studying the British government's methods of encouraging men to volunteer for the armed forces as it is a poster that would have been pasted on to a wall or noticeboard to encourage young men to join up and fight for their king and country. There is no date given for the poster but it was possibly produced before the introduction of compulsory military service in 1916 as it is designed to encourage men to volunteer. The poster is supposed to represent a time when the war is over and the young man who didn't volunteer now has a family, so he has to explain to his children what he did or didn't do in the Great War. This poster is one of hundreds that were produced during the war, and while it uses guilt to encourage men to volunteer, other posters used national figures (such as Kitchener), patriotism, hostility to Germany and other methods of appealing to young men. The government used other techniques to encourage men to volunteer, such as setting up recruiting offices in key areas and organising speeches and parades to appeal to young men's patriotism. By 1916, all of these methods were becoming less effective because the war on the Western Front had become a war of attrition with very heavy casualties.

Practice question, p38
Give a brief account of the role women played during the First World War. (4)
The large number of men at war meant new job opportunities for women, both in replacing men at the front, and in assisting with the war effort. Women were employed as nurses or ambulance drivers at the front, in munitions factories producing guns and ammunition, in other jobs traditionally done by men (drivers, ticket inspectors, secretaries and clerks), and in the Women's Land Army as farm labourers. When war broke out, most women supported Britain's involvement in the conflict. Some women tried to get men to volunteer by giving white feathers to young men not in uniform (even soldiers on leave). War work changed many people's attitudes towards women and their role in society. Many women enjoyed greater social freedom and financial independence, and their contribution to the war effort was seen as being of great value.

p40
To what extent do Sources A and B agree about French aims during the peace negotiations of 1919? (4)
Sources A and B to some extent agree about French aims during the peace negotiations of 1919. Both sources are hostile to the Germans. Source A is a French poster produced after the war, but Source B represents the views of all of the victorious allies, not just those of the French. Both sources focus on the death and destruction resulting from the German invasion in 1914, leading to the deaths of seven million by the end of the war. Source A calls the Germans 'murderers' and shows a French town in flames, while Source B says that the Germans conducted the war in a 'savage and inhuman manner'. Source A suggests that the French are worried about future German attacks and how to avoid them, while Source B lays the blame for the war squarely on German shoulders, and demands justice and compensation for Germany's victims. Neither source is able to provide evidence about the role of the politicians representing each of the victorious allies, and how their discussions modified the aims of the French during the peace negotiations.

Practice question, p41
How fully do Sources A and B describe British reactions to the terms of the Treaty of Versailles? (5)
To some extent, Sources A and B describe British reactions to the terms of the Treaty of Versailles. Both sources agree that the peace treaty made future war or wars more rather than less likely. Source A is a British cartoon produced in 1919 commenting on the Treaty of Versailles. According to the cartoonist, the children of 1940 will weep because there will be war as a result of the mistakes made in 1919, and the children of 1940 will be 'cannon fodder' or victims of war. The 'Tiger' is the French leader Clemenceau who is shown to be unaware of the implications of the peace treaty terms, and the conflict that they will cause. Clemenceau is shown to be the leader of the politicians who have drawn up this harsh treaty.
Source B is a British journalist's view of the treaty that is hostile, too. It was produced in 1929, and the journalist has had ten years to assess the implications of the Versailles Treaty, unlike the cartoonist. The journalist refers to 'vengeance', 'injustice' and 'absurdity' when speaking of the treaty in a hostile way. In particular, Source B comments on the impossibility of trying to extract huge reparations from Germany.
In 1919, there were many people in Britain who were keen to punish the Germans, and who didn't believe that the treaty terms were harsh enough. The cartoonist's point of view would not have been shared by too many people in Britain. In 1929, there would have been more people who shared the journalist's hostile view of the treaty, having witnessed Germany's problems up to 1923 and being aware of the need to revise the reparations burden imposed on Germany after 1923. Since the reparations terms had been revised, it would be logical to assume that the other terms may have to be revised in the future.

UNIT II: CONTEXT C
Practice question, p45
To what extent do Sources A and B agree about events in Europe in the years 1937-1939? (4)
Sources A and B agree to an extent about events in Europe in the years 1937-1939. Both sources agree that most people in Europe were worrying about the outbreak of war in these years. Source A is a comment made by Chamberlain when he became Prime Minister in 1937 that 'war wins nothing, cures nothing, ends nothing'. Source B is a cartoon criticising the policy of appeasement by illustrating a comment made by Hitler. The cartoonist claims that there is peace because the British and French governments have abandoned their children, in the form of smaller European states, to Nazi aggression. Often in cartoons, words mean the opposite of what the cartoonist really thinks, so Czechoslovakia, Poland, Hungary and so on cannot look forward to a Christmas of peace. The key difference between Sources A and B is that Source A justifies the appeasement policy by saying that war should be avoided at all costs, while Source B suggests that war is inevitable because of Hitler's aggression. In Source A, Chamberlain is aware of the horror and destruction brought about by war, and he is keen to avoid it at all costs. Source B points out that Chamberlain's policy means that small countries that are too small and weak to stand up to Nazi Germany on their own, cannot look to Britain and France for support. The cartoonist suggests that this policy will only make Nazi Germany stronger and more likely to attack other countries in the future.

p50
What was the Soviet Union's opinion of the Marshall Plan as shown in Source A? (4)
The Soviet Union was hostile to the Marshall Plan. According to the Soviet cartoon, since Europe has been weakened by war and destruction, as represented by the image of Death and the damaged helmet, Europeans would become dependent on American aid. The Marshall Plan could be seen as part of an American plan to dominate Europe. As far as the Soviet Union was concerned, the economic aid represented by the Marshall Plan would further develop the political and military influence of the USA in Europe. The plan's success would limit communist influence in western Europe.

Practice questions, p51
1 How fully does the evidence in Source B explain why the Soviet Union opposed the establishment of NATO? You should use your own knowledge and give reasons for your answer. (4)
Source B partly explains why the Soviet Union opposed the establishment of NATO. The Soviet government claimed that the states forming NATO were threatened by no other country or countries. There was no need for these states to act in self defence according to the Soviet Union. In fact, instead of being a threat to NATO, the Soviet Union felt threatened by the new alliance. At the same time, the Soviet Union's policies had encouraged the USA and its friends in western Europe to work closer together. The Soviet Union did not regard the Marshall Plan as a genuine attempt to relieve post-war suffering and problems in Europe. They saw the plan as an attempt to extend the influence of the USA over western Europe. Therefore, the Soviet Union opposed the establishment of NATO as it was another attempt by the USA and its allies to prevent the spread of Soviet influence in western Europe.

2 Discuss the Soviet government's attitude towards the establishment of NATO in 1949. (5)
The Soviet Union was hostile to the establishment of NATO in 1949. The Soviet government claimed that the states forming NATO were threatened by no other country or countries. In fact, instead of being a threat to NATO, the Soviet Union felt threatened by the new alliance. The establishment of NATO followed on from the other initiatives introduced by the USA and its allies to prevent or contain the spread of communism in western Europe. The Truman Doctrine and Marshall Plan were responses to the post-war economic crisis facing western Europe, and the civil war in Greece. Both crises looked likely to extend the influence of communism in western Europe. When communists took control of Czechoslovakia, western European countries formed the Brussels Treaty Organisation. When the Soviet authorities feared a revival of Germany, they began the Berlin Blockade. The USA and its allies responded with the Berlin Airlift. Soon, the Brussels Treaty Organisation developed into the North Atlantic Treaty Organisation, with the USA and Canada as new members in 1949.

UNIT III: CONTEXT A
Practice question, p59
Describe the events that led to the setting up of the Confederacy, between November 1860 and February 1861. (4)
In November 1860, Abraham Lincoln, as the Republican candidate, won the presidential election with only 40% of the votes. He had become a national figure with his 'House Divided' speech in 1858 when he attacked the institution of slavery. Many people in the slave states believed that Lincoln would attack the independent character of individual states as the first Republican President. In December, South Carolina seceded or resigned from the Union. Between January and February 1861, Mississippi, Florida, Alabama, Georgia, Louisiana and Texas seceded from the Union. In February, a provisional government of 'Confederate States' was set up at Montgomery, Alabama. Jefferson Davis from Mississippi was appointed provisional President of the Confederacy, and he established his capital at Richmond, Virginia.

UNIT III: CONTEXT B
p63
Describe how the British Raj affected the lives of the Indian population. (Note: for this answer you should write a short essay of several paragraphs) (8)
The British Raj affected the Indian population in five or six key areas. You should go on to write one or two sentences about each of these areas: education; communications; trade and economic exploitation; political and social discrimination; religious and social divisions among Indians; violent and non-violent opposition to British rule. Also, you could mention these Acts, and how they affected the Indian population of the Raj: India Act, 1919; India Act, 1935.
There is no need to write a conclusion to this type of question.

p64
How useful is Source A as evidence of non-violent opposition to British rule? (4)
This source is quite useful because it was written by an eyewitness who appears to have observed the scenes at Dandi in 1930 described in the source. The author describes the non-violent opposition to British rule that took the form of not fighting back and not shouting or raising arms to fend off blows from the police. The author was an American journalist

who may be more likely to take a neutral view of these events, and who may not be biased in favour of either the British rulers or the Indian opposition. The brief extract does not give any information on the reasons for this demonstration taking place, or the violent reaction of the police to the demonstrators, and represents only one view of that day's events.

p65
To what extent do Sources A and B agree about the non-violent demonstration at Dandi? (4)
To some extent, Sources A and B agree about the non-violent demonstrations at Dandi in that both sources make a clear distinction between the brutality of the British rulers and the bravery of the Indian demonstrators. In Source A, the British authorities are brutal while the Indians are incredibly brave. In Source B, the British authorities are accused of believing in the racial supremacy of Europeans and being determined to exploit Asians. Source A points out the dignity and bravery of the Indian demonstrators while Source B notes that Asians can look down on the English (i.e. British) after what they did at Dandi. On the other hand, Source A contains a description of the event written by an eyewitness, while Source B contains someone's opinion of the event's significance. Also, the person who wrote Source B was an Indian and is likely to be biased, while the author of Source A was an American who may be more likely not to be biased.

Practice question, p65
How fully do Sources A and B explain the growth of opposition to British rule in India in the 1930s? You should use your own knowledge and give reasons for your answer. (4)
Sources A and B partly explain the growth of opposition to British rule in India in the 1930s. Source A was written by an eyewitness who appears to have observed the scenes at Dandi in 1930 described in the source. The author describes the non-violent opposition to British rule that took the form of not fighting back, and not shouting or raising arms to fend off blows from the police. Source B was written by an Indian after the events at Dandi and the author accuses the British authorities of believing in the racial supremacy of Europeans and being determined to exploit Asians.
Your second paragraph should use recalled

knowledge to describe the extent to which the sources contain the information required to answer the question about the growth of opposition to British rule. In this case, were the attacks on the non-violent demonstrators widely publicised? Was the opinion of the author of Source B shared by many Indians? A key point from recall is how much opposition to British rule grew after 1930. You should say whether or not support for non-violent demonstrations grew or declined after this event.

UNIT III: CONTEXT C
p70
To what extent do Sources A and B agree about the White forces in the Civil War in Russia? (4)
The sources agree to some extent about the White forces in the Civil War in Russia. Sources A and B both give the names of the White generals. Both sources refer to the foreign countries involved. The cartoon shows characters representing Britain, France and the USA controlling the dogs representing the White generals. The map refers to the foreign anti-Bolshevik forces, including the British and French.
On the other hand, Source A is an example of Bolshevik propaganda and it suggests that the White generals were controlled by foreign powers. This is probably a biased point of view. Source B shows that the foreign powers sent troops and ships to Russia, while Source A shows them keeping their distance.

Practice questions, p71
1 To what extent do Sources C and D agree that the New Economic Policy was a success? (4)
To some extent, the sources agree that the New Economic Policy was a success. Source C contains facts and figures while Source D contains a man's opinion. The author of Source D was a Bolshevik, therefore his information may be biased and unreliable, making it less likely that Source D would agree with the statistics in Source C. However, the author of Source D's comments about the food shortages before the introduction of the NEP are confirmed by the statistics in Source C about grain, cattle and pig production. Source C also shows that food production increased after the introduction of the NEP. Source D describes opposition to the NEP among party members, despite its obvious success in the form of cafés opening and

restaurants and factories going back to private hands. This success is also apparent in the statistics in Source C.
2 How useful is Source D as evidence of the success of the New Economic Policy? (4)
The source is quite useful as evidence of the success of the New Economic Policy. It was published in 1992, but it is an extract from the autobiography of a Bolshevik who lived through the introduction of the NEP. As a Bolshevik, the author may be biased against the NEP, but the author does not deny that the NEP succeeded in key areas. Many Bolsheviks believed that the policy was not in line with their beliefs. The author describes the hostility of many Bolsheviks to the success of the NEP, and the fact that they were not satisfied with Lenin's justification of the new policy. The source extract provides us with an interesting insight into the reaction of some Russians to the NEP, although it is only one point of view.

p74
How useful is Source A as evidence to explain why the collectivisation of agriculture was introduced by Stalin in 1929? (4)
Source A is quite useful as evidence to explain why the collectivisation of agriculture was introduced by Stalin in 1929. It shows how backward agricultural methods could be at that time in Russia. The source shows horses being used, rather than tractors, as a sign of backwardness. However, the photograph was taken in 1923 and conditions may have improved by 1929 when Stalin introduced collectivisation. Also, the photograph was taken to show how backward agriculture was at that time, and may not accurately reflect actual conditions on a real farm. Instead, the source may be evidence of how Stalin was determined to use photographs and other types of propaganda to justify his policy of collectivisation.
How useful is Source B as evidence to explain why the collectivisation of agriculture was introduced by Stalin in 1929? (4)
Source B is very useful as evidence to explain why the collectivisation of agriculture was introduced by Stalin in 1929. The source was produced just after the introduction of collectivisation, and in it Stalin gives the reasons why he introduced the policy. These include a desire to catch up with and overtake the capitalist countries in terms of

technology. The source is probably biased, as Stalin is trying to justify the policy and would be prepared to hide any negative aspects of the policy's effects. However, this source represents the reasons given by Stalin to the Russian people to explain the introduction of this policy.

Practice questions, p75
1 How useful is Source C as evidence of the success of the first Five Year Plan? (4)
Source C is useful as evidence of the success of the first Five Year Plan because it shows that the Soviet Union believed that the success of this plan was sufficiently impressive to anger its critics in capitalist countries. The Soviet Union produced this propaganda poster to illustrate how much progress Soviet industry has made since 1928. Since the poster is an example of Soviet propaganda it is biased and exaggerates both the success of the first Five Year Plan, and the reaction of foreign observers to its results. At the same time, the poster makes it clear that the plan was introduced as much to impress foreign rivals, as it was to benefit ordinary Russians.

2 How useful is Source D as evidence of the success of the plans up to 1940? (4)
The source is quite useful because it contains statistics about industrial output in the Soviet Union between 1927 and 1940. The figures cover the production of coal, steel, oil and electricity, and these resources are useful indicators of industrial development. The figures have been put together from Soviet and western sources, so that the risk of exaggerated Soviet figures being used on their own has been reduced. The chief weakness of this kind of source is that unless you are a trained statistician and an economic historian, it is very difficult to draw useful conclusions from these figures, apart from detecting rises and falls in production. Most readers would not be able to identify the significance, if any, of a rise of two million tonnes in the production of oil in two years, compared to a rise of 35 million kWh of electricity in the same period.

UNIT III: CONTEXT D
p78
How useful is this source for studying German politics in the 1920s? (3)

This source is very useful for studying German politics in the 1920s because it identifies the main political parties in elections during the 1920s. The source shows that the SPD, Centre Party and the DNVP dominated elections in the 1920s. It is clear from the source that the Nazis were not a significant political force in national politics until after 1928. The source illustrates the fact that the German system of proportional representation made it very difficult for a single party to gain an overall majority, and close results led to coalition governments. On the other hand, since political history is about personalities, crises, decisions taken, agreements made and so on, a table of electoral statistics can only tell us so much about German politics in the 1920s.

p82
Why did Hitler change the Nazi Party's organisation and political programme after 1923? (3)
Hitler abandoned the idea of seizing power by military force. He decided to win power through building up the Nazi Party's representation in the Reichstag. In this way, he could legally gain power by winning a majority of representatives in the Reichstag. He made these decisions following the disastrous Beer Hall Putsch that meant he had to rebuild the weak and divided Nazi Party as a political force. Hitler realised that he had to attract the support of wealthy and influential Germans, and this meant revising the party's political programme and editing out most of its socialist features.

Practice question, p83
Explain why support for the Nazis grew rapidly after 1929. (8)
Check that your answer contains the six points listed for this question on page 83. Then show your answer to your teacher.

p86
Describe how Jews were treated in Nazi Germany in the years 1933-1939. (8)
In 1933, the SA were ordered to organise a national boycott of Jewish shops and businesses. Jews were sacked from important jobs (civil service, the law, universities and schools, newspapers, radio and film). The following year, all Jewish

shops were marked with a yellow star or the word 'Juden' (Jews). Jews had to sit on separate seats on buses, trams and trains, and in parks. In schools, Jewish children began to be victimised.
In 1935, the Nuremberg Laws came into effect: German Jews were no longer allowed to marry 'Aryans' (German non-Jews). Jews were encouraged to leave Germany so long as they could find a sympathetic country that would allow them to enter as refugees. The next year, after a Nazi official was shot by a Jew, the SA destroyed shops and synagogues and killed about 1000 Jews. Around 30 000 Jews were arrested. This event is known as 'Krystallnacht' (Crystal Night or the Night of Broken Glass).
Try to write a third paragraph, in your own words.

Practice question, p88
Explain why the lives of boys and girls changed in Nazi Germany, 1933-1939. (8)
Once Hitler became Führer, all youth organisations were taken over by the Nazis. Young people were encouraged to join the 'Hitler-Jugend' (Hitler Youth Movement), originally set up in 1925. In 1936, the movement had approximately 4 million members, as other youth movements had been closed down. In fact, membership of the Hitler Youth was almost compulsory for young Germans aged 10 to 18. The movement was divided into five different sections, with separate sections for boys and girls.
Boys could belong to the Little Fellows from 6-10, the Youth Folk from 10-14, and the Hitler Youth from 14-18. For girls, there were the Young Girls from 10-14 and the German Girls from 14-18. Members attended youth camps every year, and there were special schools for members who received top marks in exams called Adolf Hitler Schools and Order Castles.
Boys were prepared for military service, and children of both sexes were encouraged to report on any adults, including neighbours, teachers and family members, who made critical comments about the Nazi government.
Try to extend the third paragraph in your own words, or write a fourth paragraph.

Key terms

The following key terms focus on some of the more popular topics at Standard Grade.

International co-operation and conflict

Context B: 1890s-1920s

Armistice
ceasefire – the end of the First World War fighting

Conscientious objectors
people who refused to join the army on moral or religious grounds, sometimes called 'conchies'

Conscription
when people are forced by law to join the armed services, and possibly imprisoned if they refuse

Convoy system
merchant ships sailing together in a zig-zag pattern protected by destroyers

Going over the top
troops advancing out of their trenches en masse

No-man's land
ground between two opposing front lines, controlled by neither side

Propaganda
use of the media through songs, newspapers, posters etc. to put forward a particular point of view

Race for the sea
race to capture the Channel ports in the First World War

Reserved occupations
jobs that were exempt from conscription, such as miners, farmers etc.

U-boats
German submarines

War of attrition
to win by destroying more enemy forces, whatever the losses of one's own troops, and so wear down the other side

Zeppelins
German airships used to bomb British cities in the First World War

Context C: 1930s-1960s

Articles of the Covenant
rules that governed the League of Nations

Isolationism
policy of non-involvement in world affairs practised by the USA between the First and Second World Wars

League of Nations
formed after the First World War to help prevent another World War, similar to the United Nations

November Criminals
name given by ordinary Germans to German politicians who signed the armistice in 1918, and the subsequent Versailles peace treaty in 1919

Reparations
compensation money Germany had to pay for 'causing' the First World War

The Big Three
victors of the First World War – the USA, France and Britain

Treaty of Versailles
signed at the end of the First World War between the Allies and Germany

War Guilt Clause
the part of the Versailles Treaty in which Germany accepted responsibility for starting the First World War

Context C: 1930s-1960s

Anschluss
union (particularly in relation to Germany's union with Austria)

Appeasement
making concessions to aggressive countries to avoid war

Axis
the alliance between a number of fascist states in the lead-up to the Second World War

Blitzkrieg
lightning war

Comintern
Communist International

Lebensraum
a German term that means 'living space'

Phoney war
first few months of the Second World War when no aggressive acts by either side took place

Plebiscite
referendum or vote of the people on a particular issue

Scorched earth policy
policy of burning crops and buildings in order to deny supplies to an enemy

Ultimatum
final demand or threat

Cold War
the rivalry and tension between the capitalist West and the communist East after the Second World War

Contain
stop

Defect
flee to another country

Domino Theory
American theory that if one country became communist, its neighbours would follow suit

Imperialist
wanting to dominate the world with economic and military power

Iron Curtain
imaginary line between communist Eastern Europe and capitalist Western Europe

Marshall Plan
American economic plan for the reconstruction of Europe after the Second World War

Reparations
compensation

Satellite
client or subordinate (e.g. satellite state)

Summit
meeting

Veto
block or prevent

Warsaw Pact
treaty between communist European countries

People and power

Context C: Russia 1917-1941

Bolsheviks
group of Russian revolutionaries led by Lenin who gained power in 1917

Commisar
title given to ministers in the revolutionary Bolshevik government

Collectivisation
system in which small private farms were merged into larger state farms

Five Year Plans
plans drawn up under Stalin to speed up industrialisation of the USSR

Kulaks
better-off peasants

NEP
New Economic Policy – Lenin's economic reforms to ensure food supply after the failure of War Communism

Purges
murder or imprisonment by Stalin of leading Bolsheviks and many millions of officials and army officers

Red Army
the Bolshevik army

Show trials
trials based on little or no evidence designed to convict leading Bolsheviks during Stalin's rule

War Communism
emergency economic measures carried out by Bolsheviks 1917-1921

White armies
anti-Bolsheviks supported by foreign powers

Context D: Germany 1918-1939

Aryan
a white person of non-Jewish descent

Chancellor
head of the German government

Depression
high unemployment and mass hardship

Final Solution
Nazi policy to wipe out the Jewish race in Europe

Hyper-inflation
vast increase in the cost of living due to the devaluation of the mark

Kristallnacht
Crystal Night, or the Night of the Broken Glass, when thousands of Jewish businesses were destroyed

Nazi
a member of the National Socialist party, led by Hitler

Night of the Long Knives
purge of the S.A. (Brown shirts) by Hitler

Putsch
sudden attempt to remove a government by force